Become the Person You Dream of Being

WES BEAVIS

POWERBORN

Become The Person You Dream Of Being
by Wes Beavis

Copyright © 1994 POWERBORN
Administered by Drum Boy Pty Ltd

First Printing   3,000
Second Printing   25,300

National Library of Australia Card Number
and ISBN 0 646 15853 8

TYPESET BY
The Typesetters
7 Finlayson Street, Wollongong NSW 2500

PRINTED IN AUSTRALIA BY
McPherson's Printing Group
5 Dunlop Road, Mulgrave VIC 3170

COVER & DIRECTION BY
Wayne Larkin of The Visual Design Group
237 Berkeley Road, Unanderra NSW 2526

ILLUSTRATIONS BY
Gino Campson

PRODUCED BY
Powerborn
PO Box 192
Figtree NSW 2525 Australia
Facsimile (042) 716383

DEDICATED TO

Eleanor Joy,
my companion in love and life

The author wishes to express his gratitude to

Medford and Vina Jones
Barry and Gay McMurtrie
Winston and Joy Broad
Tom and Caryn Avelsgaard   AUSTRALIAN DIAMOND
Scott and Kim Alexander   "Rhino Success"

*The author would also like to thank
the following for their help in preparing this book*

Julie and John Cochrane
Rosanne and David Moore
Brendan and Kim Scollary
Cameron Beavis
Chris Beavis
Wayne Larkin
Gino Campson

CONTENTS

FOREWORD

WHEN I FIRST MET WES, he arrived on schedule to entertain at one of our regular business seminars. I had never seen him or heard him perform and for all I knew, he may have sung off-key: I wasn't overflowing with confidence. My decision to invite Wes was based on the recommendation of a business associate who bubbled about his performance. He told me that Wes was a talented young family man who sang a positive message with energy and passion; who made the auditorium his stage, and sang as happily on top of the chairs as he might between them. He sounded like our man!

Speaking to Wes for the first time, I quickly learned that he had a desire to encourage business people, to affirm the message of free enterprise, and to honour the value of success and family life. He wanted people of the nation to believe in themselves, their God, and their country. It all fitted our scene perfectly but he had never performed in the business arena before. He didn't even know what to charge. Then I was sure he was our man (regardless of whether he sang in tune)!

We discovered on that first occasion what you are about to discover. Wes is his own man; he IS his message. His songs, his words, and his presentation were so fresh that he literally 'got' the last words to one of his songs as he rode the elevator down to the function. We realized that night that we were taking a tiny part in the uncovering of a wonderful talent.

Since then, Wes has won the admiration of thousands for his performances and wisdom. Get comfortable and enjoy these coming pages because you, like me, are going to have a better life and business for being with him.

WINSTON BROAD
Broad & Associates

INTRODUCTION

I T SEEMS ALMOST A LIFETIME AGO but I still remember my first grade teacher calling to me from the front of the classroom. It took me a while to register that someone was seeking my attention and of the many words she said to me all I can remember was "stop dreaming and pay attention." I did enjoy the occasional journey into the realm of fantasy. To be imagining myself as a fireman fighting a horrendous fire that was threatening the school or a policeman catching the robber was a much more exciting use of my mind at the time. From the tone of my teacher's voice, I got the impression that dreaming was something you were not supposed to do.

So I grew up thinking that dreaming, apart from when you're sleeping, was an indication of a lazy mind. Try as I did to avoid it however, I was always drawn to imagine myself in scenarios beyond present reality.

It was not until years later that I understood the place and power of a dream. When reviewing the great events of my life and development, I discovered that they all began with a dream. The experience where the mind transcends the present and imagines something good becoming reality seemed to be at the start of every one of my noteworthy achievements.

Somehow, and perhaps mysteriously, dreaming is the first step to releasing reality from the realm of potential. It can unlock desire that has been laying dormant. This dream induced desire can then set you on a course to becoming what you dream of being.

When you think about your life ask yourself this question "Is the world seeing the best of me?"

Maybe your answer to this is the cause of that niggling frustration that you have been carrying. Deep inside, you know that you have more to offer than what the world is currently seeing.

Sometimes you catch yourself visualizing being someone greater. Have you noticed that when you come back to reality, the dream leaves you with a gnawing feeling that there is a greater you longing to emerge?

12

Therein lies the power of the dream. It beckons you to consider becoming someone greater. If you have a dream, you are poised for greatness. For the seed of greatness germinates in the dream. The question now is, what does it take to make the dream come true?

WES BEAVIS

CHAPTER ONE

Getting Your Best Self Forward

❦

SOME TIME AGO I was standing in my neighborhood hamburger take-way shop. Having placed my dinner order, I was content to talk to Mario, the twenty-two year old owner. My work gives me the opportunity to travel around the country a great deal and as a result, I have enjoyed many a hamburger served in many a different way. This day I was preparing to savour a favourite, the mighty Mario-burger – the best in the land and right down the road from where I lived!

As the ingredients sizzled on the grill, I ventured to compliment Mario on his unbeatable burger. His eyes lit up at first but then, as if he was under some social obligation, he threw a wet blanket over his moment of glory by making a comment that played down his capability.

He responded in a way that has become, sad to say, standard social practice. He denied himself the privilege of sun baking in the warm rays of the compliment and instead surmised that surely there were better and that I must be kidding. I wasn't.

I wished that I could have conveyed my pride in what he was doing more convincingly. I wished even more, that he believed that his service to customers was far greater than just heating food elements. There was something special about his hamburger. Eating it was an experience.

With my dinner still cooking, conversation turned to the upcoming election of politicians for the next term. I made a statement indicating some interest in the policies of one particular party. Perhaps this was a mistake. A girl standing next to me at the counter decided to get in on the conversation.

She responded to the comment I had made by saying, "That party is only interested in suiting themselves and the interests of rich people. They don't care about us poor people."

Suddenly, I wondered who was receiving the greatest amount of heat – the meat on the grill or me! It was a good time to back pedal and resume conversation about the mighty Mario-burger!

Standing there in the moments that followed, I was compelled to ponder her comment. Her tone indicated more than a half-joking dig at the public office.

Her cynicism seemed to reflect a belief that politicians of a political party were the deciders regarding the welfare of her future.

I wanted to say something. Should I go into battle? What would it prove? The last thing I wanted on my hands was a debate on politics. Not to mention, the chance of her falling, sobbing, into my arms with gratefulness for my pointing out the error of her judgement, was remote at best!

Saved. The burger was ready. I thanked Mario for dinner and headed towards the door. Yielding to the temptation to have the last say, I turned to her and said, "You know one of the things I love about this country is they've never passed a law saying you must be poor."

Granted, this girl may have been in a situation of challenge regarding her personal income. However, let's not miss the point. Nobody can force you to be less than what you decide to be.

The good news is that there is no reason why she can't improve her situation. In fact, there is no reason why she could not become a great leader of the nation – if one day she decided to put her best self forward.

Sure there are always obstacles that would stand in the way of our upward transition. However, the greatest obstacle is not anything placed there by outside forces but the obstacles we place before ourselves, for example, thinking in our minds that "this is as good as it gets". If we refuse to accept this notion, we conquer our first obstacle and begin the journey to improving our own situation.

17

Likewise with Mario. The good news is that the future can be even greater than his present situation.

I asked him whether he had ever dreamed of opening a restaurant. "You could call it Restaurant Le Mario, and have the finest reputation in town," I joked but secretly hoped I was fanning the flame of a dream in his life. I knew however, that before he could achieve anything greater he would have to start believing that he did have ability.

Sometimes this world gives you the impression that greatness is something handed out by fate. Either you're lucky enough to get it, or you miss out.

When you look at the successful people in this world, you have to admit that some achieve greatness through means not translatable to you or me. Most do not.

Most people of greatness have gained that position

not by chance, luck, inheritance, or freak windfall. Rather they became that way through making the challenging decision to become the person they dream of being. Let me say that again and this time read slowly. The vast majority of great people became that way because they chose to become the person they dreamed of being. Their lives stand testimony to the fact that we have more control over our potential for greatness than we lead ourselves to believe.

You see, while it would be convenient to let you off the hook by blaming uncontrollable events for your position in life, there are too many success testimonies that deny you this luxury. That is, people who had less going for them than what you have, who went on to become someone you desire to be.

You ask, "What's stopping me from doing the same?" The answer is you. Most definitely. There are numerous obstacles that will try and stop you in your voyage but the biggest one of them all, the one that will stop you quicker, harder, longer than all other obstacles is you. Yes ... You!

The first step to becoming what you dream of being is deciding to serve the seed of greatness calling to be watered. How many people do you know who have immense ability yet their present position in life does not utilize the best they have to offer? Could you be one? I can think of only one reason that would validate a person forever accepting a position less than what they are capable. Their decision to want no more out of life than what they're presently experiencing.

If you however, heed the voice that screams inside informing you that you're capable of much more, then the best is yet to come. The best will come when you decide to put your best self forward. Now, how do you do that?

Firstly, realize that the power needed to get your best self forward is inside you. Your first step to releasing this power is to believe in yourself. Your decision to douse the desert of self doubt with the life giving water of belief means the seed of greatness can start to grow.

I know of no one who has excelled by projecting their insecurities. Sure we all have a side to ourselves which lacks confidence, but why promote it when it gets you nowhere. You have been serving doubt for long enough. It's time to start serving belief. When you make this choice, you have commenced putting your best self forward.

Winners Start Their Own Breaks

Some people think that greatness eludes them because they haven't been given a break. This may be true. What is also true is they will probably die waiting for this break! I don't disagree that it's nice when someone "parts the Red Sea" for you, but these miraculous breaks happen so rarely that you are unwise to depend on them as the key to releasing your potential.

Though you haven't been handed a break, you can still get ahead and in doing so increase the chance of gaining a break in the future. In fact, the key to getting a break is starting it yourself.

When I was going through college I worked at a fried chicken fast food outlet every Friday and Saturday night. Cooking chicken may be someone's dream for their life but it wasn't mine.

Three thousand, five hundred pieces a night. Not a job you bragged about. Yet, it was the only one available and that was because most guys weren't willing to work those nights. Friday and Saturday nights were prime party time and the members of the 'party set' said I was mad for taking it.

They were right. I was madly intent on paying my college fees knowing this would expedite graduating with a college degree so that I would never have to cook chicken for a living again in my life!

Upon obtaining my degree, I left that chicken shop for another town to start my profession.

Some time ago, I happened to pass that chicken cooking place of previous employment. Ten years had transpired and much personal growth had taken place since resigning. It seemed crazy to think that was how I used to spend my Friday nights – especially in the light of just having flown back from a wonderful Friday night performing a concert at an entertainment centre. It was hard to believe that unlike my chicken cooking days, my income was now being provided through something which was a dream come true.

A wave of nostalgia took possession of the steering wheel and before I knew it, I was inside the place ordering dinner. It was late at night and being the only customer I found myself in conversation with the guy who was fulfilling the role of shift manager.

I told him that ten years ago I had worked there as a cook. He nodded as he continued his stock-take of the potato salad. I went on to tell him that while I cherished the income, it did not extend to enjoying the work. To this he gave a hearty nod, his expression giving away the fact that he felt the same about his job. Conceding this however, I went on to say that even though I didn't like the job, I stuck at it knowing it was helping me get to the point where now I gained my income doing something that I loved. He was now listening intently. This was my cue to spring into encouragement mode.

I asked him if he was planning on making his current position a career. To that he replied that it was just helping him pay his way through university. That was the lead I was looking for. Enthusiastically I responded, "Then you have a dream too. You want to do something greater with your life!" He said, "Yeah I hope to ... touch wood". A puzzling response. What has touching wood got to do with him achieving his goal? Nothing.

His future was going to be better because he had a dream. Nurturing the dream into reality inspired him to go to university. His effort at university was helping him unlock his potential. He was getting his best self forward.

When you take any step to help release your potential, you are actively involved in getting your best self forward.

Someone once said, IF IT IS GOING TO BE – IT IS UP TO ME! Whoever said it, and whoever says it, is right.

I know of many people living in exile waiting for someone to come along and bestow upon them the break of a lifetime. The reality is very few of these breaks are ever handed out – if any.

Sure, every successful person attributes elements of their success to those who have helped them along the way – given them a break so to speak. Often though, it was their initiative to get in motion first, that placed them in a position of being noticed along the way.

If it's going to come true, it's up to you. Not your bank manager, your wife, or husband, the lucky break, or any other person or thing that comes to mind. Stop waiting for a break. Start your own!

What activity can you embark upon as the start in your movement toward your goal? Remember the start that you make is the start of your break.

You're An Unrepeatable Historical Event

Capitalize on this. There is no one on the planet quite like you. Stop comparing yourself to other people. They can never be quite like you so why should you try to be like them. This is a very liberating truth.

One day I found myself sitting in a picturesque place overlooking some mountains. It was the ideal environment encouraging my thoughts to rise above the tyranny of the domestic. It led to a time of personal evaluation.

For years I held back from pursuing a personal dream. My hesitancy was based on a fear that my persona was not right compared to others in the industry. A fear that I had the wrong image. As if my ability to contribute was dependent upon my image being like everyone else's! What a potential killing trap. I am grateful to God for rescuing me from this trap. In my mind I heard him say, "Wes I made you special. Your desire to copy everyone else is starting to irritate me!"

The words of Dr. T. Garrot Benjamin speak to this tendency of humankind: "We're all born originals but we die copies."

That day, overlooking a beautiful mountain setting, I made a resolution, a resolution which changed my life forever. No longer was I going to apologize for my inadequacies when compared to the strengths of others. I would forget about what I didn't have and do the very best with the strengths I did have. I resolved to quit making excuses and to start making progress.

I have never regretted making that resolution. That day I started life again.

All those who make this resolution find themselves ushered into the joy of uniquely contributing to the world in which they live. A unique contribution because, while others may be similar, none are the same.

No one else can contribute quite like you can. The world waits in patient silence but nonetheless in need of what your uniqueness can offer.

Your journey will lead to success; not as a result of how you do compared to somebody else as real success is never measured by how you do compared to the effort of someone else. You are a success when you overcome each obstacle that stands in the way of your drive to develop your dream.

Stop thinking that in order to be a success you have to be the same or better than everyone else. Start believing that you are unique and believing in the fact that there are people out there who will benefit from the uniqueness of your contribution.

What is Fear??
What is Failure?
I+ hurts.
Realizing you most
Find Another —
Better — way To
Fulfilling your
Dreams.

Beat the Fear Of Failure By Having One

One of the greatest obstacles that stops people getting their best self forward is simply this – the fear of failure.

I would be stretched to find a psychologist who would disagree with the notion that fear stops even the most brilliant, talented people from achieving their potential. Basically, the tendency of people is to think that failing is the worst thing that could ever happen to them. We fear what can hurt us and this makes us afraid of failure. The unfortunate byproduct of this is that we hesitate from venturing beyond the safe zone for fear of making a mess. Yet when you examine the life of anyone who has achieved greatness, you'll soon discover that they did it by building on what they had learned from their failures.

What I have discovered is one of the best ways to combat fear of failure is to actually have a failure. That's right, have one.

Think about this for a moment. When you are in the midst of experiencing the demise of something you have put your hope in, you feel like your world is going up in flames. However, when the smoke clears, you do discover that even though you may have lost, you still have many things left including the added wisdom from having learned from the experience.

Does a failure strip you of talent? No. In fact a failure gives you the added knowledge of how not to do it next time! The net result is your talent is actually refined.

Does a failure strip you of the ability to think? No. Nothing stops you from thinking "well, that didn't work but there's every possibility that next time it might!"

Does a failure make you go blind so you can't see a need anymore? No. As long as you're still breathing you have the capacity to see people in need of something.

Does a failure strip you of dignity? No. The most revered people in society are the ones who triumphed over the abyss.

Oh yes, a failure may set you back, but it can never break you unless you give it permission. In fact a failure, far from breaking you, can actually make you.

A friend of mine graduated from university at a time when there was an over supply of teachers for the positions available. Sandra graduated without much prospect of getting a position. This didn't deter her from sending off applications. After a while the responses came back in the form of rejection letters. To be precise, seventy six letters of rejection. She knew because she kept them in a special file.

I asked Sandra why she kept them. She replied, "I kept them because I believed one day an acceptance letter would arrive. When it did I could get my file out and remind myself that one victory is all it takes to make seventy six failures irrelevant."

Sandra developed an awareness that failure, while it may stop you for a while, is destined to lose the fight against persistence. Given time, persistence always generates a victory to triumph over failure. Sandra has since gone on to be very successful in business. I am not surprised.

There are those who would say that a person can only take so much rejection before they give up. Well, that may be true. Let's also give the positive side to failure. It can be the world's greatest refining process. It helps you cherish that which you achieve because you have had to overcome so much to obtain it. It deepens your resolve by helping you realize that while failure may hurt, you do survive it. It is often the process which helps you search and find a more suitable approach.

When you survive, you realize that failure is not the terminator of future possibilities that you once thought it was. Indeed, it can even help you refine the process of making your dreams come true. Look at a failure in this light and you are well on your way to becoming the person you dream of being.

CHAPTER TWO

The Big Picture
The Little Picture

❦

IT WAS the evening of my college graduation. My family
had travelled across the country to share in the special
event. It was one of those memorable nights which came
accompanied by the type of euphoric feeling that one experiences infrequently over a lifetime. Sure graduation cere-
monies have never rivalled the excitement of Broadway.
This one was an exception; it was mine.

Waiting in expectation for the call of my name, I
flicked through the mental file called 'the college years'. I
recalled how nervous I had been about leaving home and
travelling to the other side of the country in pursuit of education. I quickly relived the anxiety leading up to the first
set of exams, the second set, the third ... losing count at
fourteen. Not to mention surviving four years of campus life
and food! And lest I ever forget, the experience of working
Kentucky Fried weekends to pay for the privilege. My excur-

sion into memoryland was interrupted. My name was called.

As I stood, my older brother beside me at the time, tucked a business card in my hand. Heading toward the platform, I glanced at the message he had written on the reverse side. It simply read: "Wes, success is a journey not a destination."

At the time I wasn't quite sure what it meant, but the days following brought to light the impact of this truth. This night was the celebration of an achieved goal. Receiving the diploma was recognition that I had reached a passing status. Even though the likelihood of this actually happening had been queried often enough, graduation now stood declaring my success. However, in light of the message my brother had given me, was graduation declaring more than this? I had always viewed graduation as the successful end and never gave much thought to it also being the invitation to a new beginning.

The morning after graduation I woke up thinking, what now? Was my life at the present as good as I was going to get? Something inside seemed to indicate the best was yet to come, that life's engine was just getting warmed up. I started to imagine, in view of having conquered the previous unknown frontier, what else there was to accomplish. Great things that, up to now, I had never entertained possible.

While pondering these thoughts, I felt the vision of a new dream being unwrapped in my mind. It dawned on me that graduation was as much about being an invitation to start the next unknown frontier, as it was a celebration of surviving the last. This experience developed my understanding that success should not be seen as a specific point but as a continued journey on an upward trajectory. Success is a lifetime of graduations.

Each quest successfully survived elevates you. From that point of elevation, you start a new challenging climb. Remind yourself that you are not starting all over again from the bottom. Absolutely not. Your climb starts from the finishing place of your previous victory. It is a climb you could not have started had you not successfully finished the last one. You have graduated! Success is a journey where you are always graduating.

Part of the purpose of past success is that it forms the foundation of future success. The secret to getting your best self forward is to employ this principle. Build on your achievements. With what you learned from yesterday's achievement, tackle something new today. Stop and think about this for a few moments.

Having accepted this, you have to examine the activity that is presently consuming your time. Evaluate whether it is an activity that is on track with helping you become the person you dream of being. You see, what you tackle has to be constructive in helping you get to where you want to be. Otherwise, while the activity may be deserving of merit, it is a diversion stopping your pilgrimage to your dream coming true.

Self improvement is great. However, some forms of self improvement will not necessarily help you become the person you dream of being. For example, striving for a black belt in karate may be good self improvement, but is it going to help you achieve becoming a dentist if that is your ultimate dream?

Those on their way to becoming the person they dream of being incorporate two different modes into their thinking; the big picture and the little picture. It is extremely important to have both.

If you only ever thought in terms of the little picture, you may still improve yourself but you don't capitalize on your achievements. It's like the map of your life consists of thousands of little one day trips. Each trip is terrific but none really builds on the previous trip. Your ultimate destination is the place where you started.

On the other hand, if you only thought of the big picture, you will probably lead a frustrating life because nobody becomes the person they dream of being overnight. Your big picture may be honourable, possible and worthy of pursuit. Yet it may be too big a goal to achieve quickly and the chance of demoralization is high when progress is slow.

In my mind, there are four types of people. Firstly, those who have no picture. Needless to say, they do not amount to much. They have no dream to beckon them upwards. No one becomes great by accident. Without a picture on which to focus, there can be no aim and without an aim, there is no direction in which to travel.

Then there are those who think in little pictures. Fine people. Generally they live for the pleasure of the day rather than the fulfillment of a greater tomorrow. A nice life but a life that misses out on exponential growth. The celebrations later on in life are no different to the ones experienced earlier.

Then there are those who think in big pictures. Dreamers. You will often hear them say, "One day I'll ..." Time passes however, and still there is no tangible indication that the dream is emerging to become real.

Then finally, those who think in both big and little pictures. These people can often surprise you. They are not reputed as geniuses. They weren't born into it. They didn't make a big song and dance on the way through. In fact, they seemed pretty average. But there is nothing average about what they have accomplished. How did they do it?

These people simply have a big goal. A destination of grandness. Having this vision in place, they then set up a course of little goals that build on one another. Little goals which are headed in the direction of the big goal. The big picture comes about by successfully completing a series of little pictures.

Giant Leaps
And Small Steps

I learned the value of this principle when I was nineteen. A moment of wild abandon led me to decide to ride my bicycle from the city of Sydney to Brisbane, a city one thousand kilometres (621 miles) north.

With a few days training behind me and a heavy laden bicycle beneath me, I set out on this journey full of enthusiasm and expectation. It was about mid afternoon on the first day when I pulled into a service station for a drink. The going had been a little harder than I had first imagined, but I was keen.

The service station attendant, while attending to my beverage order, noticed my laden transport and enquired of my destination. Without thinking, I told him the grand and ultimate journey's end. He looked at my bike, looked at me, then laughed.

Walking out of the station I thought to myself, I know it's not a stroll in the park but I'm not trying to swim up the Niagara Falls either! Why did he have to laugh? I mounted my bike knowing that the next leg of my journey now had the burden of an extra piece of baggage – the weight of his skeptical laughter echoing around in my mind.

That night I pulled out my map certain that I must have travelled an impressive distance. I was horrified to discover that in map terms, I had travelled one inch! It seemed so insignificant compared to the distance I had to travel to reach my goal.

Day two was worse. After a solid night of exhaustion induced sleep, I sprang into action to meet the new day. My body stayed on the ground. It told me that if I thought of putting it through another day like yesterday, I should think again. My sore bottom was leading the revolt. Finally, I convinced my body not to call in the unions and to give me another chance.

My road map was not three dimensional. I had failed to notice that what lay in the middle of this day's journey was the biggest mountain range in the state. Some cars never make it.

Thankfully, I made it despite one mountain road having fourteen bends all uphill. Before each bend, I prayed that the road around the corner would begin a downhill run. It wasn't to be. Or at least not before I slipped into a state of semi-coma.

Day three. Let's not talk about it.

Day four. I decided to quit. After several consultations, the map gave no encouragement. The goal seemed as far away as it ever did.

My plan was simple. I would ride to the train station in the next town, book a seat for myself and my bike and head back home. The next step in the plan was to not tell anyone about the trip. This would alleviate the burden of explaining my failure.

Coming into town, I stopped at a roadside diner. I ordered some milk and a pie for lunch. Then I asked the girl behind the counter if she could tell me where I could catch the train.

She was the most dithery fourteen year old girl I have ever met. She kind of sang the directions:

"Well, you go over this road ... then you head down until you see a fork in the road ... um ... let's see ... then you follow it down and take your second or third right ... um ... no ... at the fork in the road you go ... um, just a minute ... (screams to back room) maaarrrther, to catch the train ... do you go right or left at the fork ... oh ... right ...

okay where are we up to …?"

I said thanks and walked outside thinking it's easier to get to Brisbane! At least I knew what direction that was!!!

Once outside, I made myself a seat on the concrete. I spread my map out on the ground before me and while eating my pie I prayed, "God I've had enough. Take me home … to heaven. Now would be a good time!"

As I sat there, a gust of wind blew across my map causing a section of it to fold over. I didn't notice at first but what happened was the map had closed in such a way to reveal only the name of the town I had marked as my destination for that night.

Interesting … as it made the map look more encouraging. The destination for that night did not look very far at all compared to the distance I had already come.

I decided to get back on my bike and head for that town and not even think about anything beyond. It was as if my focus had closed down to consider only that which was immediately before me and nothing more.

I made town that night. The next morning, reaching for the map which I had left in its partially closed state, I carefully folded it back to reveal a little more of the journey but only enough to reveal the name of the next town. What was beyond that was of no immediate interest. This became my daily practice.

The seventh morning will never be forgotten. I rode

over the crest of a hill and before me stood the beautiful sky-line of Brisbane. Riding towards the city, feeling like a champion, I spontaneously started singing the theme to Sylvester Stallone's Rocky Movies. Motorists were intrigued at this singing cyclist. Becoming aware that they were look-ing, for a brief moment I felt embarrassed. What were they thinking? Then I realized it didn't matter. You see most of them were on their way to the city to claim another day at the office. I was on my way to the city to claim victory. I had made it!

Reflecting on the journey days later, I wondered why the fourth, fifth, and sixth days were not as hard as the first, second, and third. Was it because the last three days I had become fitter? No way, physically I was exhausted from the second day on. Was it because I got my second wind on the fourth day? No, I got my second wind three hours out of Sydney. It lasted twenty minutes.

What I discovered was that my decision on the fourth day was actually the beginning of a mental strategy. A strat-egy which got me through. A strategy that has helped many people to achieve what seems impossible. On that fourth day, I decided to set my mind on the immediate task at hand and nothing more. You see when I was constantly monitor-ing my progress according to the end goal, I was becoming discouraged by the slowness of my progress.

Looking back on it now, I realize that the role of a big

picture goal is to act as a reference for direction not to act as a reference for distance. In my particular situation, as long as my small picture goals (the towns of rest for each night) were in line with the direction of the big picture goal then achieving the big picture was inevitable.

At nineteen, I learned that GIANT LEAPS ARE THE ACCUMULATION OF SMALLER STEPS.

What is your big picture vision? You are on this planet for more reason than to be born, breathe, pay tax, create ninety thousand tons of garbage, then die. You are unique. There is NO ONE on the face of this earth the same as you. Therefore, the way is clear for you to do something unique. There is a giant leaping capacity inside you waiting to do something incredible. Will you put your best self forward? Take the first step, dare to dream.

Have you got a dream? Did you used to have a dream? Whatever has buried your dream is not worthy of the exalted position it has commanded. At this point, you might be saying, just a moment, my dream was to sail around the world solo. I have a wife and children now and my dream is no longer possible. Could it be you have concluded wrongly? You can expand your dream to include them! Circumstances may refine your dream and make it even better.

Brush the dust off your dream. Stoke up the desire to dream again and drive to develop it by taking small steps in the right direction.

Is your dream to get a promotion? Then what small step can you take to put you in a better position for recognition. Then, having achieved that step, build your next step on the success of the previous and so on. One day you'll have that promotion.

Is your dream to be an actress? Go to acting school. Oh, what's that I hear? You can't afford it. Therein lies your first step. Set up a special bank account that is designed to discourage tempting plunders.

Is your dream to return to the weight of your wedding day? I have seen that dream come true for people. Set your goal. Determine the first step. Then focus on achieving your first step and nothing beyond. Remember, the ultimate goal is your guide for direction not your reference for distance lest you be discouraged by the slowness of progress.

Success is as much surviving the journey as it is reaching your goals, for the former will lead to the latter. If your pathway is in line with your destination, and you don't quit, then the achievement of the goal is inevitable.

I remember the testimony of a person of great achievement which included the phrase, "after fifteen years I was an overnight success". I thought he was making a joke but what he said was true not only for himself but many others as well. At times, I wish this wasn't the case. That instead, greatness was impatient with passing time and came sooner rather than later.

The inventor and founder of Kentucky Fried Chicken was in his sixties when his efforts brought riches. Colonel Sanders hit the goal about the time that most people retire. I am happy that persistence paid off for him but to be honest, I would prefer not to have to wait that long! I am sure you agree.

However, to view greatness in this light is to be seduced into thinking success is the destination. I have known people who never achieved fame or fortune but they never gave up on the journey to realizing their dream. Upon realizing one dream, they unwrapped another. In the process, they developed greatness in themselves that would have never surfaced had they not started the journey at all.

Sure, the rewards of this journey may bring fame and fortune, but don't be confused, they are not the hallmarks of greatness. These are the hallmarks of greatness: surviving the journey, its obstacles, its disappointments; getting back up and brushing the dust off the dream; allowing the setbacks to refine your dream; determining a pathway of small goals that lead to big goals, and being determined to get your best self forward. That is greatness and that is what makes you great.

CHAPTER THREE

Follow Through With The Do

❦

A SONG WRITING FRIEND OF MINE wrote a song titled, "Can You Go The Distance?". A line in the song states, "every mountain looks so inviting until the day we have to climb." The imagery he uses succinctly highlights a factor in human experience that I am sure is familiar to all of us. Adventure is an attractive concept until it comes time to actually step outside our comfort zone in its pursuit.

I can relate so much to that. It brings to mind the memory of a decision I made to embark on a new adventure. When I first made the decision, it seemed an exciting thing to do at the time. However, as the day for action drew nearer, the more the idea changed in my mind from being exciting to down right scary. My anxiety peaked the night prior to the start of the adventure. I spent the night vomiting!

I am glad that my anxiety prior to a new challenge does not always manifest itself this way. Nevertheless, stepping out into unfamiliar territory is always accompanied by some feeling of nervousness and apprehension. I am sure you can identify with this. I have come to recognize these feelings as indicators that one is on the threshold of entering a personal growth zone.

Feelings of apprehension always accompany people who step out of the comfort zone. Initially these feeling make you feel insecure. This is where the real danger lies. Preconceptions of the upcoming discomfort cause many to turn their backs on the life changing challenge that lies one step before them. What happens to these people? Nothing. That is just it; nothing exciting ever happens to them. They stay safe in the comfort zone, only ever thinking about doing something new and exciting. They talk, dream, maybe even wish, but they never actually taste the sweetness of new experience because they never FOLLOW THROUGH WITH THE DO! You probably know a few people like this.

You hear them say, "Oh, I might do this … or I might do that … or one day I'll try to do this … or I really should give it a go … and wouldn't it be good to do that." But for all their talking about doing something, they never actually do anything!!!

It's not that they're lazy. It's just that they want to avoid insecurity. I can understand that but ultimately it is a disposition that robs them of the possibility to become greater than what they are at the present. To never 'follow through with the do' increases the probability that later in life you may live with regret that you didn't try harder to realize what you dreamed of becoming.

One of my jobs during college was as a groundsman at the local retirement village. It taught me as much about life as my college course. After a few weeks of lawn control, I noticed that whenever I ran my mower past one elderly man's unit, he would come out and watch.

One day, I noticed he was crying. I stopped the mower and talked to him. He told me how much he had loved working outdoors when he was younger, and how much he lamented no longer having the capacity to even mow the lawn.

Mowing lawns was certainly not my idea of a good

Follow Thru with the "Do."

time, but I understood what this elderly gentleman was saying. The rest of the day I thought about what he had said, "If I had my life over again I would be less cautious and more adventurous ..." He said some other profound things which I've forgotten, but I will never forget his inspiration. A few weeks later, I was again mowing past his unit. This time, I noticed people packing up his possessions. I knew what that meant.

If there are few legitimate arguments against the value of doing something new to enrich ones life, then why doesn't the population throw themselves eagerly into following through with the do? Well, here are some reasons.

Some people feel that their ideas are not really earth shattering innovations. Sure, it may not take off like McDonald's Restaurants, or a cure for cancer. Don't let this stop you because there is someone, and maybe even a lot of someones, who would benefit by what YOU DO. Given a chance to evolve, an idea may become a shattering innovation. One thing is for sure, you'll never know unless you have a go.

Some feel that their plan isn't really that grand compared to what others have produced. That may be true but I don't know of any songwriter whose first composition went to number one in the charts; or whose first play was taken to Broadway; or whose first story was made into a movie; or

When it comes to Success in Life, "EASY" is not an Option.
BJS.

whose first design won a housing industry award; or whose first speech was to the United Nations; or whose first laboratory experiment created a cure.

Everyone of greatness has stories of humble beginnings. That's what makes them great. They realize where they have come from and what it takes to get where they are now. They know it didn't happen by accident, and while the scenery on their journey may be unique to them, they know their experience has one thing in common with all others. It started by deciding to emerge from the comfort zone and do something. Who knows what could eventuate if you decide to do the same?

Some hesitate because they cannot ensure a successful outcome in what they do. My younger brother keeps telling me, "Wes, no chance, no dance!" He's right. I never went to my high school homecoming dances because I was too scared to ask a girl to accompany me. You are only young once and with regard to this, I now carry the burden of regret.

Some hesitate because it looks too hard. They're right. It is hard. But you're always richer for the experience. When I listen to the testimonies of great people, I hear them say that what they cherish the greatest, they've worked the hardest for. How does the proverb go? A lazy man sleeps soundly – and goes hungry!

Some get discouraged because they don't get the acclamation for their efforts like they hoped they would.

Recognize where People are at in their lives; But, Focus on where they can be.

They respond by terminating further efforts. How do you know the next attempt won't be the one that breaks the drought and gives you what you hoped for?

Others prefer to avoid the possibility of the embarrassment of making a mistake. No argument here! I don't like living with past errors any more than you. But if you had the choice of being known for successfully doing nothing or having made a few blunders along the journey of doing something significant with your life, which would you prefer?

The Blessing From Blunders

A friend of mine once said, "I've learned more through my failures than through any of my successes." If this is true then surely the effects of failure are not totally negative.

Don't worry I'm not going as far as saying we should prefer failure and embrace it as a wonderful friend!! My preference is still to avoid it. However, some time ago I came to a point in my life where I realized I wasn't failing enough. My scar count was not that high. In other words, my lack of scars told me I wasn't really pushing the limits very hard.

I was given a book called 'STORMS OF PERFECTION'. The author, Andy Andrews, wrote to famous people asking them to tell the story of their greatest failure. Many of these people accepted the opportunity to share and

DESTINY - your destiny - is not a matter of Chance; it is a Matter of choice - 50 the Decisions you have made in your life that put you where you are Today.

the basis of the book was born. A novel idea, a collection of failure stories as opposed to success stories.

I was amazed to read of the failures and hardships that these famous people had borne in their pilgrimage to the top. Finishing the book, I thought about what past experience I would have contributed to this book had I been asked. The truth was that none of my failures were that impressive. My failures seemed far less compelling in the light of their stories. It was then that I realized, I was playing it too safe and not risking enough.

The common theme that ran through all their testimonies was how their failure had been a refining process, enabling them to become the people they dreamed of being.

Failure is not something to be sought after but every person of greatness has savoured the experience! Most of them say that surviving the failures gave them the strength to handle the success when it eventually came.

That book encouraged me to charge out of the comfort zone. I have had greater successes because of it and I now have a blunder story worthy of inclusion in any book on failure! The amazing thing is that I lived despite its awfulness. Previously, I lived in fear that a blunder of that magnitude would kill me – it didn't. I survived. I actually feel a little stronger.

Rejection Is Inevitable And Very Profitable

Nobody appreciates being rejected. Many escape the risk of rejection by deciding to do nothing that would expose them to the possibility. Their rationale is 'why stick your head up if there's the chance it will be kicked?'

The truth is, if you want to do something significant with your life, you must stick your head up. Commit yourself to a course of action. Be seen to be doing something with your life. If you do this, you will be criticized and rejected by some. Let me reiterate BY SOME ... but not all. The great news is that some people will be so grateful that you have come across their path; they will appreciate you in a way you wouldn't believe!

When I think about the most magnificent people

who have walked the face of this earth, Jesus Christ is one of the best. Now, when we consider how much criticism and rejection he faced then you and I have no chance of escaping the odd bit of scorn! So, don't think that the ones who make it are the ones who are above being criticized. The ones who make it are the ones who get on with the job despite being criticized.

The liberating point is that for as many critics as there may be, there will be many who rejoice in what you are doing. Go with the rejoicers rather than the knockers. A friend of mine sums it up this way, "Don't let the dissenters be the deciders!" It is true. Don't let your great progress be thwarted by the least worthy person in your world – the critic.

Never let the negative person knock you off course. They are not worthy of that power of influence. Instead, think about whether they can help you shape your course. Let me explain with an illustration.

When I started out as a musical performer, I was tyrannized by even the smallest amount of criticism. My goal was to have my songs and performance loved by everybody. This led me to do things that weren't really me. It was an effort to impress people that would only have been impressed had I been a large-lunged and full-bodied Italian, or a heavy metal musician with an earring through my nose. Pleasing everybody was impossible.

One day a personal decision was made; I would maintain a commitment to being flexible and courteous but ultimately I was going to be me. I reminded myself that for as many who didn't appreciate, there were those who did. All I had to do is go with those who were appreciative.

That is all it takes. Go with the ones who would go with you. Leave the rest to be picked up by someone else. If you don't, you can spend all your energy trying to win the regard of someone who you will never impress at the cost of missing a thousand people wanting what you have to offer. Employing this principle means you will be more discerning of where you invest yourself. You won't waste valuable time, energy, and emotion trying to convert the staunch rejecter.

To understand this is very liberating. Rejecters can actually, by default, help you define your market. Experiencing rejection makes you more discerning about which market you decide to target. The result is that you throw less of your pearls before swine. Or if you prefer, you throw less of your seed on hard ground and more on soil with great potential for a good yield. It is a very profitable principle to employ.

Just Do Something

Wherever you may be, however little you may have, however much you have, whatever they say, and whatever the odds just do something to get your best self forward!

Some time ago I thought it would be a good idea to come up with a poem that would help remind me of this concept. Inspiration sometimes comes when you're in the most inconvenient places. I was on a plane when inspiration for my poem came and with not a scrap of paper on me, I scribbled the words on the back of an air sickness bag. Since then I have committed the poem to memory. I also carry a little notebook in my wallet!

Referred to as my personal creed of action, this is my creative reminder. I share it with you as a summary of the concept I have explained in this chapter and also in the hope that it may water a seed of inspiration in you to develop your own creed.

I Have Decided

I have decided
To do something
My plan may be grand, or just barely stand
I may help the planet, or just one person on it
I may be a success, or learn from my mess
But with God's help I've decided
To do something

I have decided
To do something
I may run with the breeze, or crawl on my knees
I may be applauded, or go unrewarded
I'll do all that it takes
And I'll make mistakes
But with God's help I've decided
To do something

WES BEAVIS

CHAPTER FOUR

Never Quit
On Your First No

❧

M Y FATHER taught me this valuable lesson early in
my life. He was the preacher of a young church in
the remote city of Perth, in Australia. As the number of
people attending grew, so did the demand for someone to
lead the youth activities. It had been in the hands of volun-
teers but the job was becoming too large and really needed
the benefit of someone's full time attention.

Having trained for youth work in United States, a
young man named Kent took up the challenge by travelling
to Australia to help out. The church people, excited in antici-
pation of his arrival, proceeded to organize a welcome party.

Kent's flight to Perth was planned: fly from Chicago to
Los Angeles, from Los Angeles to Hawaii, from Hawaii to
Sydney and finally from Sydney to Perth. To make things a little easier my father, attending a conference in Brisbane at the
time, would fly down to Sydney and join Kent for the final leg

of the journey. Since I lived in Sydney, my job was to pick Kent up from the international terminal on the day of his arrival and take him to the domestic terminal the next day. Simple.

The next day I was woken earlier than usual by the telephone. It was Dad calling from Brisbane asking whether I had heard the news headlines. He went on to inform me that the aircraft refueling technicians at Sydney Airport had gone on strike. All aircraft were grounded. It meant none of the airlines were flying in or out of the state. Dad could still fly to Perth as he was in another state and therefore, unaffected by the strike. However, Kent was stranded. He would miss his own welcome party.

This is when the fun started. Dad told me to call the airport, explain our situation, and see if anything could be done. Knowing the efficiency of a union ban from previous occasions, I thought this was a pointless exercise but decided to call if only for Dad's sake.

As could be expected, the phone lines were jammed. Finally, I succeeded in getting through. I quizzed the booking attendant as to the possibility of the strike being called off prior to Kent's booked flight. "No chance," he said, "they're really digging their heels in this time. We'll be lucky if it's over before the weekend. Sorry, there's nothing I can do ... click."

I called Dad and broke the news saying, "You'll just have to fly to Perth without him and cancel tonight's welcome party." Dad wasn't ready to give in. He asked me to call the airport and try again to see if there were any other options. I said, "Dad it's hopeless". He insisted.

It didn't work. The same answer, "Sorry Mr Beavis, we understand your situation, but everyone is stranded. There's nothing we can do." Well, that should satisfy Dad, I thought. It didn't. He asked me to call again. In exasperation I said, "Dad, don't you know when to quit?" He asked me to trust him. (Don't you hate it when they ask that?!!)

I got back on the phone and once again, wrestled my way through a barrage of engaged signals. Finally, I was connected then promptly put on hold! I remember wondering while I waited whether all Dads are like this or just mine? Then a booking attendant came on the line: "Yes Mr Beavis, how can I help you?" This guy sounded too chirpy on a day when all airport officials could be excused for being grumpy and abrupt. I carefully explained our situation. He tapped away on a computer keyboard while he listened. His manner gave me hope. At least if there was any way possible, he seemed the type of person who would do his best to find it.

"Can you hang on a minute?" he asked. Moments later he came back on the line with some good news. He said that they were working in conjunction with private aircraft owners to help get stranded people on their way. He went on to say that he could get Kent on a light plane to Newcastle.

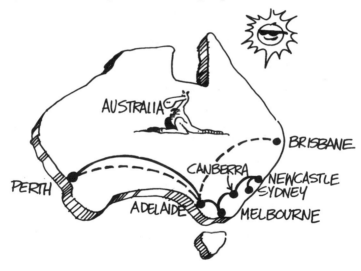

Great, I thought sarcastically. Newcastle was 200 kilometres (125 miles) north of Sydney whereas Perth was 4,600 kilometres (2,900 miles) west! I was wondering how this guy got a job in travel when his voice broke in: "Then ... um ... from there I can connect with another light aircraft flying to Canberra." I got the feeling that he was enjoying the challenge of putting the odd shaped pieces together.

60

He continued: "Then, I can get him on a major domestic carrier to Melbourne." I said, "Wait a minute, I thought the major domestic airlines weren't being refuelled in this state?" He informed me of something that I had completely overlooked. Canberra, while being geographically in the state, is its own territory. It wasn't affected by the strike!

"From Melbourne I can connect him with a flight to Adelaide. From Adelaide I can connect him through to Perth. In fact, I can re-route your father's ticket from Brisbane so that he flies to Perth via Adelaide. That way they can fly to Perth together as planned."

IT WAS POSSIBLE!! But at what cost? Surely I had clocked up a few thousand dollars in all this. I grimaced at the thought of how embarrassing it would be to bail out because of the cost, especially after all his hard work and the kindness he'd shown. The inevitable had to be asked, "How much extra are all those flights going to cost?"

"Twenty five dollars added to the existing pre-purchased ticket will be sufficient," he said.

Calling with the good news of the miraculous breakthrough I said, "Dad, you were right to keep trying. I finally got through to someone who made a way possible."

I will never forget what he said, "Wes, it doesn't always work out as good as this, but one thing is for sure, NEVER QUIT ON YOUR FIRST NO."

Since then, I have employed this principle into my behavioural repertoire. It has worked in my favour time after time.

You see, sometimes the word NO doesn't represent the extent of impossibility, but rather, the extent of difficulty in getting to the point of possibility. Put more simply, sometimes "no, it's not possible" really means "yes, there might be a way, but it will require extraordinary effort to find it, and I couldn't be bothered!"

My wife, Eleanor and I married just prior to her last year of teacher's college. Our desire for cohabitation led to a decision that she would have to transfer to a university near where I was working. No problem. We travelled to the university to enquire about the transfer procedure.

The young man at the desk proceeded to tell us that the university would only grant Eleanor one year's credit for the two years already done at her current university. This I thought was unfair since the course was the same. And Eleanor wasn't exactly thrilled by the exchange rate!

"I want to talk to the admissions manager," I said, thinking that the manager might waive university policy as a kind act of goodwill towards a student from a rival university. Nice try! She did little more than repeat what the office clerk had already said. She did say, however, that we were free to make an appointment to see the Head of the Education Department although stating at the same time, "I don't think it will make any difference."

We made the appointment. The day came and we had dressed to impress, knowing that we wouldn't get a second chance on a first impression. The department head was nice but a little vague. I was hoping we'd leave his office with the keys to the university, instead all we walked away with was the name of a Mr McClellan. Another person to see!

Mr McClellan was the giver of hope. He told us if there was a way, he would find it. Getting in contact with Eleanor's current university staff, he worked out an arrangement whereby Eleanor could take certain subjects at the new university which would be accepted as fulfillment of what was required to finish the course at her current university. A scenario we hadn't even envisaged as a possibility. It worked out even better than a transfer. Eleanor graduated with her friends from the school where she had commenced her course.

It turned out that indeed there was a way. Someone just had to find it. It was possible and, in this instance, neither parties were compromised in the process. Often, that is the case. How many breakthroughs are never experienced because the first no is accepted as final? Never quit on the first no. It might be that the next person you contact becomes your Mr McClellan, the one who gives hope for a breakthrough.

You will recognize this person when you find them because they will say, "it may be difficult, but if it is possible, I'll find a way."

The Pathway of Least Resistance is Short ... And Goes Nowhere Special

When you decide in your mind that you are going to do something with your life, ready yourself for the fact that you have chosen to go the pathway of much resistance.

Not only will you experience occasional criticism, not only will you experience apprehension and nerves, not only will you sometimes fail, but there are also people out there who will tell you it is not possible. Sometimes those people can be declaring that message from foreboding positions.

When someone says, "No, it can't be done." They might very well be right. But there is always the chance that they may not be right all the time.

Ready yourself for occasional resistance. Keep in mind the saying of Zig Ziglar: "If you wait until all the lights are green before you leave home, you'll never leave home."

There will be obstacles along your journey to becoming the person you dream of being. It is how you respond to these obstacles that often makes the difference. If you quit the first time an obstacle presents itself, then you will never relish the joy of having made it despite them saying you couldn't. Not to mention you never becoming what you dreamed of being.

You see nobody achieves greatness without the help of a special added dimension to their personal strength. I call it the T factor.

What is this T Factor? How do I get it?

It's called tenacity. To triumph over an obstacle gives it to you. The tenacious person is less likely to be intimidated by a problem and is more likely to hold together despite the pressure to break apart. They are voted most likely to succeed because they are more persistent. They are easily identifiable in a crowd because they are the ones doing something extraordinary with their lives.

You are not born with this quality. You can't inherit it. You can't buy it. You can't win it. You only get it by collecting the white flags of surrender from the obstacles you have personally triumphed over.

Isn't it great to know this? It has nothing to do with muscular strength, wealth, beauty, or being born on the right side of town. It has everything to do with what we do with the lives we have.

Vision Blocking Mountains Can Also Be Platforms For Greater Vision

Whenever you conquer something that has been a challenge to your advancement, you grow by it. You are never quite the same after a victory as you were before. When you overcome an obstacle in your pilgrimage, it opens your eyes. You see possibilities that you could not see before because the obstacle was taking up all your view.

I knew a girl who was unsure about what she wanted to do after high school. There was no enthusiasm for that time frame at all. At first, I thought it was a lack of motivation and vision. Knowing Sarah could have a great future, I was left puzzled by why she was like this.

A few months later, I noticed a great change in her.

She had gusto and exuded a confidence about the future that wasn't evident before.

I questioned her about this and she said it was all due to night school. It turned out that all along she had dreamed of training for a specific profession. To gain university entrance to train for the profession, she knew it required a certain score in her final exams. That was the problem. She was doing adequately in all her subjects except one. Yet it was the one where poor performance would knock her out of contention for gaining the score she needed.

Sarah's lack of enthusiasm for the future was due to the fact that she couldn't see past the difficulty this subject had posed: "How could I get excited about university when I felt I couldn't even pass high school?"

Someone told her about the same subject being offered at night school. She went along and discovered the way the teacher taught the material made the subject come alive. She testified to how the night school class not only helped her grapple with the subject, but it renewed her confidence about passing the course and achieving university entrance.

Standing on this confidence, Sarah could see the possibility of attending university was very real.

Your excitement about the future may be stifled by an imposing obstacle. But when we overcome that obstacle, we find ourselves personally elevated. Along with that elevation comes a new confidence. A confidence which compels us to look further into the world of possibilities.

To be sure, there will be times where our passage is ultimately blocked by a no. But let's not surrender on the first one. Never quit on your first no. Never finish if at first you fail.

There I stand in the face of a mountain
Thinking surely there must be another way around
And I'm sure I hear this big ol' mountain laughing
Saying you will never make it off the ground

There I stare at this big mountain
Knowing there's an even bigger one locked up inside
And something says that the one in front isn't moving
'Til I push this one called doubt out of my life

So I move in the name of adventure
The only thing I leave is my shadow in the comfort zone
And as I climb I feel myself getting stronger
'Cause somehow the journey's made me grow

And as we climb we are lifted
To discover wonders in the realm of possibility
For once this mountain blocked us in our vision
But now it is the ground from which we see

WES BEAVIS & BILL RISBY

Lyrics from the song HOPE RETURNS written by W. Beavis & W. Risby as recorded on "When We Believe" © 1993 POWERBORN administered by Drum Boy Pty Ltd. Reproduced with kind permission.

CHAPTER FIVE

Court The Thoughts That Support

❦

T HE ABILITY TO CHOOSE the thoughts we think is one of the greatest powers available to us. We all have it and what's more to the point, we all underestimate it. When we learn of its power, we discover it has the ability to make us ... or break us!

Early in our lives, school provides us the opportunity to fill our minds with information. As important as this information may be, it is not enough to ensure success in life. Success is determined by how we control our mind in regard to information. When we control our mind, we control the power of the information. Until we develop this ability, we tend to be controlled by the information.

Growing up, I was told sticks and stones will break my bones but names could never hurt me. To be honest I preferred getting beaten up if I had the choice between that and being the recipient of verbal humiliation. Physical bruises healed a lot quicker than mental bruises, some of which I carried for years. Information, if we let it, can control us. It certainly did for me in this instance.

Sometimes it is very hard to avoid listening even if the information being transferred hurts us personally. And it doesn't stop there. If we admit the damaging information to our memory, we give it the power to hurt us again and again. For once a hurtful thought is given permanent occupancy in our minds, it feels compelled to keep raising its head from time to time to justify its place.

Every day we are bombarded with negative information. The only way to avoid the damaging effect of negativity is to stop it taking up residence in your mind. You filter it. You have the right to manage your mind. What you think about is your choice. When you choose to ponder information which lifts your spirit, you are being empowered. On the other hand, if you choose to ponder information which troubles your spirit you are being 'depowered'.

If you want to keep moving upward in life, then keep your foot on the accelerator and off the brakes. When you invite the thoughts that support into your mind, you are putting your foot on the accelerator. Thinking about thoughts that drag you down is like putting your foot on the brakes, it slows you down. It makes getting to your destination that much slower.

If you are "Empowered" you will grow. And become The man or woman you DREAM of Becoming.

If you are NOT edified you will be Diminished... And Become the LESS- of the MAN or woman you could Be.

You can surround yourself with People who will be on your "Balcony" — cheering you on and lifting you up. OR, you can allow people in your "Basement" to criticize — and pull you down. The Choice is yours.

Court the thought which supports because time spent pondering a thought that drags you down is just not worth it. If you find yourself investing time and mental energy on a negative thought, ask yourself if the investment is helping you reach your potential. When you discover that it isn't, you discover it is clearly a poor investment.

My little boy is growing rapidly. He is not even giving me a chance to develop my wise old dad dimension. He is picking up knowledge quicker than I can plan a strategy to teach him. The other day, after he had been bathed by his mother, he escaped her clutches to take a quick lap around the house in the nude. Running into the kitchen with the cheekiest grin on his face, he looked at me then pointed at his male part and said, "Pee Pee." I can't remember teaching him that!?! But at eighteen months, he's worked it out. Maybe I better start preparing that father to son talk sooner rather than later!

Well aware that there are no guarantees of outcome when it comes to parenthood, I just hope that when he 'leaves the nest' he has developed the understanding that the guards to his mind are in his control, that he can choose what goes in and what stays out. For every mind is a bank and the state of the balance is determined by whether the transactions engaged in are positive or negative.

The secret to developing an empowered mind is exercising control over what thoughts you deposit and entertain.

Evaluate each thought that presents itself for admission at the reception desk of your mind. At that point determine whether the thought is going to be a constructive tenant or a destructive one and screen those "tenants" accordingly. Do this and you are developing your mind to be the greatest asset for helping you become the person you dream of being.

Take From The Past Only That Which Can Help You In The Future

There was a time a few years ago when I found myself in the role of listener in a counselling situation. A young father had exploded in response to what seemed a minor situation. Minor as it was, it served as the detonating spark to a mind highly charged with suppressed emotion.

Before long, I was caught up listening to him recount situation after situation of past hurts and disappointment. It was obvious that he had taken great care to store each of these memories in his mind. The way he described each detail indicated to me that he periodically recalled each bad experience, as if he were brushing the dust off it so he would not forget even one horrible detail.

I didn't know where to start, or whether it was right for me to start unravelling the complex issues. As serious as they sounded, I knew they were just symptoms of a deeper illness and I was out of my depth. He needed help from someone more qualified and I made the appropriate recommendation. One thing I did know was that harbouring the negativity was serving to feed his mental malignancy. Dare I say, it probably caused it in the first place.

75

If the thought is going to drag you down, it's not worth carrying around. How many people do you and I know who are slowed down in this life because they carry with them unnecessary burdens? There are times we've carried a few ourselves!

In the Bible, God recommends his devotees to forgive their enemies. You can be excused for wondering why because it does seem to mean the enemies get off the hook. Well, that maybe so but God thinks of it this way: their life is already messed up by hurting you. Therefore, it's no use your life being messed up as well by carrying around thoughts of bitterness, anger, and resentment. These thoughts are heavy and will weigh you down rather than lift you up.

A mentor of mine apologized to me one day for a fifteen minute conversation that he had with me the previous day. He had basically spent a little time recounting how another person had tried to verbally assassinate him. It had a happy ending because the culprit shot himself in the foot in his assassination attempt. I was puzzled as to why he was apologizing. The story was true and the third party got all he deserved. He said, "That may be so, but it was negative and therefore, such a waste of energy."

I went away thinking about his comment. Basically, he was drawing attention to the fact that he used up 30 minutes in cumulative time (fifteen minutes of his time in telling the story and fifteen minutes of my time as listener) celebrating a negative. He considered that a waste of energy. I admire him for that and still have much to learn from this mentor.

Our pilgrimage along the road to becoming the person we dream of being is difficult enough. When you consider the obstacles, inclines, injuries, and bad weather, all of which are things beyond our control, why would we want to make the journey harder by carrying burdens that we have the freedom to leave behind?

Of the barrage of thoughts that apply for entry into your mind, only admit those which will help you in the future.

My father died suddenly when I was twenty four. He was my best friend and I am grateful for the life he gave me. I remember coming back to the family home about a year after his death to help pack up his study. Having had many degrees conferred upon him, he was a learned man. His study was his castle. It was jammed with enough books to start a college library as well as files of all sorts. Actually, he hardly threw anything away if he thought that it might have value in the future.

Having packed most his books away, I discovered something that I wished he had thrown away. In the back of a lower drawer of his filing cabinet was an unmarked file. People in leadership, whether it be in public, private, or religious fields, sometimes receive letters of complaint and dissatisfaction; letters that express disappointment about the leader's decisions or their style or manner, or any one of a number of possibilities. It doesn't matter how fantastic a leader is no one ever escapes the odd negative letter. I have received my fair share of mail like this but mine went straight in the waste paper basket. Dad kept his in a file.

There were no real letters of malice but then again, there was enough to inflict pain upon any heart. I imagined how hurt he must have been to receive them. I don't know his reason for retaining the letters but I wished he hadn't. Mail like this ultimately serves to drag one's spirit down and nobody needs that! They're just not worth their weight carrying them into the future.

I decided that day to start a letter file of my own but not for collecting letters of criticism. I still discard such letters promptly. Instead, it is for letters of encouragement. I call it my victory book. Every letter that gives me a lift gets glued in! Every now and then, when the burning light of my self esteem needs extra fuel, I get the victory book out and have a good read about how wonderful I am!

VicToRY BooK = LeTTeRS oF EncooRAgemenT

An Empty House Is Not An Option, Choose A Good Tenant!

There is much that happens to us in the course of a day which would give us fair reason to think negatively. If this wasn't enough cause for concern, it seems that negative thoughts flood into our minds with greater ease than positive ones. For some reason, thinking negatively comes more naturally.

However, when I survey the field of champions, I discover no one has ever become great by allowing their minds to become incubators of pure negativity.

I have heard some people espouse the virtue of having an open mind. Yet the greatest people I know don't have open minds, or closed minds, or negative minds. They have positive minds.

Our mode of consciousness demands that we ponder on something. If we don't condition our minds to court the thoughts that support, the opposite happens. Have you ever noticed how easy it is to start dwelling on the negative things without planning it that way? Oh, it may start out as an innocent little niggle, but if allowed to, it can drag you into a condition of anxiety.

The best way a farmer can minimize weeds taking hold of his field is to plant the field with crop bearing seed. The same can be said of our minds. The best way to eliminate a negative thought is to substitute it with a positive one. To leave the house of our minds unoccupied is not an option. If we don't install a good tenant, we welcome a bad tenant by default.

Negative thoughts are like pirates searching the seas for a vessel to sabotage. The onus is on us to avoid negative thoughts being pirates which sabotage our minds. The best strategy is to have one's mind filled with positives, leaving no room for negative visitors. In the event that you catch yourself being seduced by a thought that is dragging you down, think about a positive thought that you could substitute in its place.

Seek Higher Help

I remember reading something Dr. Norman Vincent Peale said in one of his books: "There are some things which get into our mind that we don't have the power in ourselves to deal with." I believe what he says to be true. My own experience bears testimony to that.

Many times, I am able to pull my mind into check. That is, discern a thought taking hold which is pulling me under and then ponder on something positive to once again make my spirit buoyant.

Then, there have been other times I have gone to the "bank" and found it overdrawn. I haven't had the strength to perform the task of substitution nor the knowledge of something positive to substitute. It is then I realize the need for higher help.

I find my higher help in the pages of the Bible. It speaks of a God who cares and offers that which I cannot create for myself.

When the future looks uncertain, I read one of his promises: "Those whose hope in the LORD will have their strength renewed. They shall mount up with wings like eagles; they shall run and not be weary; they shall walk and not faint."

To fill my mind with this thought, brings a peace which is hard to explain but it works. When I am feeling lonely on the journey, I read another promise: "Be sure of this – that I am with you always, even to the end of the world."

Any person who dares to dream has experienced times where reality fails to meet expectation. When this happens, you are left with a gap between what you hoped for and that which has transpired. Sometimes the reason for the shortfall is beyond our control; other times it is related to our competency. However, regardless of the cause, somehow you have to deal with this gap.

You can fill the gap with excuses, blame, self-pity, envy, or one of many other destructive thought processes.

Ultimately, these thoughts bring no peace and still leave you with an unreconciled shortfall. Those who have experienced the peace of God say that it displaces the negative emotional garbage that filters into the gap and gives you a mysterious capacity to cope with the gap. If your expectation is plausible, then higher help will empower you to make up the shortfall.

Some feel that it is too fantastic to believe in a power beyond. Others appreciate the sense that though they walk by themselves, they are never alone. For me, the following verse has always been a source of uplift.

Footsteps

One night a man had a dream.
He was walking along the beach with the Lord
and across the sky flashed scenes from his life.
In each scene, he noticed two sets of footprints in the sand;
one made by him, and the other by the Lord.
When the last scene of his life flashed before him,
he looked back at the footprints in the sand.
He noticed that many times along the path of his life
there was only one set of footprints.
He also noticed that it happened at the worst times in his life.
This bothered him very much, so he asked the Lord about it.
"Lord, you said that once I decided to follow you,
you'd walk with me all the way.
But I've noticed that during the times of trouble,
there is only one set of footprints. I don't understand
why you left me when I needed you the most."
The Lord answered,
"My precious child, I love you and would never leave you.
During your times of trial, when you see only one set of
footprints, that's when I was carrying you."

M. R. POWERS

CHAPTER SIX

Provision Flows To Vision

❧

NOT A DAY GOES BY where we are not given the wonderful gift of opportunity. A time of favour given where we have the option to do, develop, and achieve something. Making the most of our opportunities helps shape who we become.

The person who lives in regret says, "I should have done it when I had the chance. Had I taken advantage of the opportunity when it presented itself, I could have avoided this remorse."

A few years ago Eleanor and myself enlisted the services of a building company to build our home. As the builders were in the construction process, they gave us the opportunity to include some extra drainage under the house. On rare occasions, underground springs were known to form during long periods of wet weather. The recommendation was only a precaution in the unlikely event of a spring forming. I decided to save the money and took the gamble that the "unlikely event" would not occur. It did.

Every time it rained, we experienced major flooding under the house. After four years of trial and error, I finally solved the problem. Yet, not without sustaining the regret that I could have saved a lot of time, headaches, and money had I done something when I had the opportunity. In this case, I backed away from the opportunity because it brought with it a complication, a demand on already tight finances. Opportunities do this; that is why we are often cautious in the face of them. While bringing the promise of blessing, they also introduce new obstacles to be navigated.

So why bother? Because every opportunity taken and every obstacle survived elevates you into greatness.

OVERCOME

Grand Opportunities Sometimes Never Make It To Your Door

When I think about my pilgrimage and the opportunities that served to change my life, hardly any of them knocked at my door! Oh, I heard them calling from across the street. Sometimes they beckoned from clear across town. Sometimes they presented themselves from a different state. Most times, I found them when I left the house intent to hunt them down from their place of obscurity. In fact, I just can't recall any of my greatest opportunities knocking at my door. Something inside told me that the most helpful opportunities had to be actively pursued. When I did, I found them. You will too.

Now, getting motivated to pursue opportunity is very difficult. That is, unless you have a reason for doing so. However if you have a dream, then that's all the reason you need!

A vision for where you want to be in five years time will stimulate you to get on the move. Once you're on the move, you start to run into opportunities which will help you realize that vision. Some will come in the form of signposts pointing you in the right direction. Others will become the very break you need to achieve your goal. When this happens, you have experienced the power of a great principle in your favour. That is – PROVISION FLOWS TO VISION.

I have experienced this law so many times that it has revolutionized the way I move into the future. I used to shy away from challenges until I felt I had all the reserves reckoned necessary to well and truly cover the voyage. This turned out to be a slow way of getting anywhere.

Now, I'm more inclined to commit myself to the journey even though I don't have all the resources needed to get to the destination. I do this in faith knowing that provisions will present themselves, by way of opportunities, along the way. They always do.

I have vivid recollections of leaving home at eighteen, bidding farewell to my family and boarding a plane bound for the other side of the continent. It was time to start training for my chosen profession. An exciting time but I had one problem. All I owned in the world was with me. It consisted of two suitcases, two guitars and a bank book with a balance of eight hundred dollars.

College fees for the first year were two thousand five hundred dollars. The college administration required you to pay one semester in advance. With only eight hundred dollars in my possession, I couldn't even pay for my first semester!

My parents, almost bankrupted in the process of raising four teenagers, were not in a position to finance me. Besides, when I left home, I was staking a claim to independence and was proud of it; a position which is hard to claim while still being financially dependant on your folks!

Standing in line with other students waiting to see the college administrator, I contemplated a strategy of how to explain my inability to fulfill the payment required. In my nervousness, I struck up a conversation with another student enrolling for the first time. Hoping he was in the same predicament as me, I broached the subject of fees.

He motioned me to come closer, as if to indicate I was about to be privy to some classified information. "I have twelve thousand dollars in the bank", he said, "I was just wondering whether I should just pay for the full four years right here and now, and be done with it." Great, just the encouragement I was looking for!

Could I have been more prudent in my financial preparations for college? Well, maybe but I knew it wasn't necessary. Yes, when I got on that plane, I was flying off into much uncertainty but there was one thing of which I was certain – my vision of what I wanted to become. It stood solidly fixed in my mind. Something told me this was all I needed.

As long as the passion for your dream keeps your vision in place, the journey towards it will provide the opportunities needed to get you there. Prior to the journey, you may not know where they come from or how they'll come but they're out there somewhere. If you are on the move toward your goal, you are in a position to catch the wind when it blows.

When the DReam is BIG enough, the Facts don't count.

The opportunity I needed was a job. I found it. The college course ended up costing over eleven thousand dollars. I came to college with eight hundred dollars and a dream. It was more than enough.

The Returns Never Arrive Before The Risk

Performing in concert is a lot of fun for me. Catching up with the audience after the show, one to one, is part of the enjoyable experience. I remember one particular post-concert conversation with a guy who asked for an autograph. He told me that he wanted to do what I do. He asked me a question that I have often been asked, "How do you get started as a performer?"

It is a hard question to answer. I wish there was an easy answer. Something that goes like this: well, first you get a degree in music, then after graduation present yourself to a record company and apply for a job as an artist. Nothing could be further from the reality!

I have a sneaking suspicion that when people ask me a question like that, they are looking for a specific route. A step by step plan that gets you the job in the end. If I have a formula it is this – take the plunge and make it up as you go along; have a vision and then don't expect a return until you've risked yourself in action.

The returns never arrive before the risk. That principle is spoken of in the Bible and proven true by the experience of millions. Unless a seed of wheat falls to the ground and dies, there will be no harvest.

Decide on your first step and then take it. Commit yourself. It doesn't need to be a planet stopping step. In fact, it is better if it is a smaller rather than a larger step but still large enough to drag you out of the comfort zone.

When you discover along the journey that opportunities pop up to help you achieve each step, you discover for yourself that provision flows to vision. What a discovery!

My friend, determine your first step then take the plunge. When you emerge triumphant, award yourself a gold medal. Then determine your next step. This time you will have the added benefit of previous success to encourage you to bite off a little more than before.

Never Surrender Your Course To A Lack Of Resource

Some of the greatest plans have been terminated by the words, "we don't have the money!" In most cases whoever says it is absolutely right. But, if the idea truly has merit then the pursuit of it will stimulate the needed resources to materialize.

Remind yourself of the saying: "where there's a will, there's a way." Sure, it may be difficult but it still may be possible. Never let a momentary lack of resources terminate your dream.

I remember being on tour and experiencing a bout of sickness. I think they call it love sickness. My tour schedule had been such that I had not seen my wife for what seemed a long time. All it took was Cliff Richard's version of the song "These miss you nights are the longest" playing on the Hi-fi of my heart to influence the Love Doctor in me to prescribe a spontaneous mid-tour trip home.

My schedule gave me a two day break before my next performance. Eleanor was 880 kilometres (546 miles) away. No problem, I was thinking as I called the airline: "Sorry Mr Beavis, all flights are full. It's school holidays you know."

Not to worry, I thought there is more than one way to get from point A to B: "I can sleep on an overnight bus and be there in the morning." Not to be. For the same reason, all buses were full. I called the train station, "Sir, you're in luck. There's one spare seat on the last train out, but it leaves in fifteen minutes, can you make it?" I was at least forty minutes away from the station. Not likely.

I felt beaten but my vision of a two day break with my family wouldn't let me give up. After persistent effort, I landed a ride with a truck driver who was driving his prime mover in my direction, and in fact, happened to be going through the very town where Eleanor was staying. Without deviating from his route, he was able to deposit me within a thirty second walk of the front door. Though not as quick as a plane, it was a journey I will never forget and the two days with my family was worth every effort in getting there!

A Dream Will Draw Water Out Of A Dry Well

Have you ever discovered something that really appeals to you but you haven't got the amount needed for its purchase? It happens to me all the time. What astounds me is that once I set my mind on getting the item, the funds begin to materialize. The commitment to obtaining the desired acquisition helps me channel my finances better. I set up a budget. It helps me stop the flow of finances slipping through my fingers like it does so easily when I have no real reason to be saving. The goal seems to lubricate the mind to help it tick over what can be done to raise the finance. Possibilities come to mind. Funds can be realized by liquidating possessions no longer used. Resources can be raised by taking advantage of opportunities to increase income. Supply can be obtained by cutting back on current overheads.

Nobody I know has a money tree. Even the millionaires I know have liquidity challenges due to having their wealth tied to investments. But what you will notice in life is that if people catch a vision which excites them, they rearrange their priorities. Before you know it, the rivers of resource that were pretty dry before, start to flow again.

A friend of mine named John told me one day that he had bought a block of land. It was something that Eleanor and myself wanted to do, but knew we couldn't pursue the idea because we didn't have the money.

John proceeded to tell me how much the block cost. It was very cheap. "Must be in a bad location," I thought. When asked where it was he said 'the Heights'. WHAT?!! That was the best suburb in the whole city in our view! Eleanor and myself had dreamed of living there for years.

It was late at night when John told me, so I determined that in the morning I would march down to the real estate agent and enquire as to the availability of these 'cheap' blocks.

As planned, there I was talking to the land sales agent. I don't know why, because we hardly had a few hundred dollars in the bank! The agent said that the land developer was wanting to open another stage of land release but was restricted from doing so until all the blocks of the previous stage were sold. It turned out that there were two blocks left so he was letting them go at a never to be repeated price. My friend John bought one. I decided to buy the other.

I called Eleanor at work and asked if I could take her on an excursion during her lunch break. She loved the block of land but posed the inevitable question, "Honey, how will we buy it without a deposit?"

As we were both earning an income, I knew that we could obtain a loan from the bank to purchase the land. However, before the bank would consider our loan proposal we needed to demonstrate our credit worthiness by having a deposit. It was finding two thousand dollars to enable us to pay the deposit that proved the obstacle. Yet, the excitement of being on the verge of a dream coming true demanded we not let this opportunity pass. We felt there had to be a way.

Enthused by the excitement of a dream, priorities were reorganized. Each having a car, we agreed that to help make the dream possible we would sacrifice one of them. Getting a second car down the time line was going to be easier than finding another block of land. It is amazing what inconvenience one is willing to entertain when you sense a dream materializing. We sold a car and made the deposit.

Many times, it will come through unexpected means but nevertheless, provision always flows to where there is vision. Each time it does, you and I move on from the experience greater than we were before.

CHAPTER SEVEN

Pay Back
What You Borrow

❦

THE YEARS OF HIGH SCHOOL introduced some new challenges. Most of them could be summed up with one word – girls! Until age thirteen, I had rarely considered the purpose of the opposite gender but that summer something happened. Something that was to change human history. At least mine.

Returning to school after a wonderful summer vacation, I headed into an unexpected shock. The girls I had once shared the classroom with had now become women. How could one summer holiday have evoked such a shapely transformation? How come my internal radiator was no longer cooling the heat in my engine? A crisis arose. That day, I developed a new way to carry my school bag. Guess I had changed too!

Being made alive to the splendour of the opposite sex, myself and a few school buddies discerned the need to position ourselves better. That is, position ourselves so that we would be noticed by the recipients of our new found interest. We decided the best strategy was to become school jocks, a term of endearment for school athletes. It was the season for track and field. So we joined the track team.

The week prior to the first track competition with another school, the coaches had all but finalized the runners for each event. There were a few races vacant and they used me to fill one that was not as highly regarded as others – the eight hundred and eighty yard dash. I wasn't even sure what the event entailed. My instructions were to wait until the sound of the starter's gun then run as fast as my legs could take me twice around the track.

The gun went off and so did I. Expecting everyone to be running faster than they were, I assumed the front of the pack. By the end of the first two hundred yards, I had well established my dominion over the rest of the field. I remember thinking, "This is great! This is my type of race. This is looking good for a resounding victory." I visualized myself being awarded the first place ribbon. I imagined the pride of winning much needed points to assist our team's overall competition tally, not to mention becoming a hero in the process.

As I was powering along, elated with the discovery of a latent talent, something tragic happened. I 'hit the wall'. It was as if my feet stepped into boots of concrete. In a moment, without warning, my body fatigued. I tried to rally myself but no amount of positive self talk would re-inspire my body to perform. One by one each runner passed. Rounding the last bend, I saw the race was over for everyone except me. Humiliated, I staggered across the line and then collapsed on the inner field. What a way to impress the girls!!??

That day introduced me to a new lesson in life – if you want to go the distance, you must pace yourself.

Pay Back What You Owe To Yourself

Your body is the mechanism that carries you and your dreams around. Sometimes people abuse themselves in the drive toward their dream. What is the use of that? If you wreck yourself in the process of achieving your dream, you're left with nothing to carry you on to enjoy it. Doesn't that defeat the purpose?

Of all the race events that attract attention, the marathon is perhaps the greatest. The origins of the marathon race go back to a war between the Athenians and the Persians in what is known as the Battle of Marathon. Prior to the battle, the threat of the mighty Persian army caused the Athenian commanding general to send a request for back up. He sent Pheidippides, a young athlete, running to Athens and Sparta to deliver the message.

The distance Pheidippides ran was one hundred and

forty miles. He ran with haste and determination. He succeeded in arriving to deliver the message, then he collapsed and died of exhaustion. He achieved his goal. We can't argue with that but it did cost his life.

These days, while the marathon is still hallmarked as a test of human endurance, the risk is not considered as such a risk to life. We watch a marathon race without thinking that the runner is flaunting themself in the face of death. Rightly so, because due to the preparation of the athletes, the race is not so much a death defying feat.

While the physical cost to an athlete of this race is nonetheless extremely taxing, they have developed ways to make the run a little easier. In other words, they have devised ways to run awesome distances and live to tell about it. Let me draw the parallel between their race and ours.

Firstly, long distance runners keep the weight of their attire down to the bare minimum. They only carry into the distance what is going to help them. Anything that weighs them down, they know will reduce their chances of reaching the goal. When we COURT THE THOUGHTS THAT SUPPORT, we employ this principle. We know the drive toward the goal is hard enough so we think carefully about what is to be carried on the journey. Some things left behind will lighten our load and make our journey easier.

Secondly, marathon runners have points of refreshment along the way. At various places along the course, the runners pass a refreshment station. Someone holds out a cup of fluid. The runner grabs the cup, gulps that life giving juice down, and continues the race. It replenishes that which they have used up. They know that if they do not replace the energy and fluids used, the body dries up and dies.

We are no different. I am all for going at a cracking pace towards the goal. Yet, if you do not occasionally stop and replenish what you have used, then you will dehydrate. At best, you may stagger across the line but it may be at a cost which draws the validity of the achievement into question. At worst, you could collapse and never run again. You have to PAY BACK WHAT YOU BORROW. It is one of the foundational principles that life is built on.

This principle has been illustrated in many ways. Dr Stephen Covey in 'THE SEVEN HABITS OF HIGHLY EFFECTIVE PEOPLE' says that you must occasionally stop to sharpen your saw; it makes the task of cutting easier and therefore, you accomplish more in the long run.

Isn't that the issue – being there for the long run? It is no use reaching your goal if the process turns you into a carcass, leaving you unable to build on your success.

A successful businessman and good friend of mine gave me one of his secrets to his staying power in a professional field where casualties are high and expected. He said, "Wes, sometimes you just have to lay back in the saddle for a little while." When I think about it, even God rested on the seventh day. Who am I to argue when He suggests we do the same?

Points of refreshment along the way are imperative to going the distance. These rejuvenating refreshments come in many shapes and sizes. Their refreshment value will be determined by the type of person you are. What experiences refresh you? Think about it. How long has it been since you have felt refreshed? Are you in need of replenishment now?

One of my very simple refreshers takes place about once a week. I go to the movies. Usually, while everyone else is working (this really adds to the sense of holiday about it). I take an extended lunch hour and attend a midday matinee. This practice costs me about the price of a cheap set of golf clubs each year. For me, it's worth it. It's one of my points of refreshment.

A time of rejuvenation is like opening a window in your life. It is a point where a refreshing breeze can blow in.

The person who says to me, "I haven't had a holiday in five years" is a person who has surrendered their lives to the control of something else. It will eventually burn them out, if not take them out – of life itself! While there are many things worth working hard for, very few are worth being a martyr for.

Evaluate your life regarding this and build a strategy for taking in refreshment. You will find yourself going even greater distance than you imagined possible by doing so. Your mind and body have inbuilt gauges which signal you when your fuel is low. When we attempt to defy the gauges, albeit sometimes for reasons seemingly beyond our control, we pay a price. We may achieve the goal but lose a life in the process.

A holiday, an inspirational conference, a camp, a retreat, a weekend away from home, a movie, the theatre, the gym, a swim, a walk, a picnic, a sabbatical, a vocational exchange with a colleague in another country, a day sitting on the top of a mountain – just sitting! I feel refreshed just thinking about the ideas!

One of these rejuvenating experiences may be waiting to recharge your batteries. Take the opportunity as an investment in going the distance.

Pay Back What You Owe To Your Family

I was privileged recently to have lunch with a senior citizen couple. In the course of table conversation, I asked them what things helped them attain forty nine years of marriage. The wife said this, "When we married, we married for better or for worse. Although nobody would desire it, the worse sometimes comes but we found together we could always make the situation better." When I heard her say this, I borrowed a pen and wrote it down. It impressed me as a profound testimony to the value of companionship.

In our endeavors of reaching personal goals, the ones we love are often our greatest supporters. Yet, amidst the heat of our determination, sometimes they are taken for granted. I must constantly remind myself not to let the tyranny of the urgent overshadow those who are ultimately more important. This doesn't always come easy, but you soon motivate yourself to alter your course when you consider the possible repercussions of the alternative.

A movie I enjoyed was one starring Steve Martin and John Candy titled 'TRAINS, PLANES, AND AUTOMOBILES'. In it, John Candy plays the part of a shower curtain ring salesman and Steve Martin plays the part of a high flying business executive. Although there were some great lines in this comedy, I have forgotten them all except the one where John Candy turns to Steve Martin and says, "The finest line a man can walk is between success at work and success at home." It probably fixed in my mind because it so accurately sums up the constant challenge facing the achievement oriented person.

Nobody ever achieves greatness without it being born out of cost and sacrifice. Of this, you need no reminder. But how much consideration do you give to the fact that the cost and sacrifice always spills over to touch the ones closest to us? They end up sharing our burden and often without us realizing it because we are so embroiled in the burden ourselves.

If you have family, it is quite likely that they also pay the price throughout your pilgrimage to becoming the person you dream of being. This is not necessarily a bad thing. A family is brought together by sharing; even if this sometimes means sharing in sacrifice. But there is a limit. There has to be points of refreshment along the way for them too.

To give them the joy of refreshment is to reward them for their loyalty and support in the face of challenge. To PAY BACK WHAT WE BORROW to the ones we love means we can proceed in our mission, without sabotaging our family in the process.

There will be times where we call upon the ones we love to sacrifice some things for the sake of the cause. Do not take for granted however, the fact that your family does not have the benefit of your dream-inspired, all-consuming fire. The reality is that they often hang in there by the nails of their love, loyalty, and trust in you. While they are supporting you in your quest, still it is initially your quest, not theirs. Therefore, to a certain degree they bear a greater load. They need to be commended and rewarded. Never afford yourself the selfish luxury of forgetting to pay back what you have borrowed.

Eventually, what you have embarked upon must pay some dividends which you can disperse to your family. Paybacks to those who support your endeavors is vital to helping them to see sense in the sacrifice. Otherwise it is too easy to ask "what's the use?" What profits a man if he gains the whole world but loses his family? A parody on another famous piece of advice!

Some parents live to serve their children. This is wrong. It is going to the other extreme. It stops your pilgrimage of personal growth and gives your children the wrong impression of life.

I have seen wonderful ability stifled in people who have made themselves servants to the lives of their children. What they fail to see is that their children need to see their parents experiencing a life of continued personal growth. If you become your child's 'beckoned call' parents, you set them up for a crisis later on in life when they leave the nest to discover the world is not at their beckoned call.

My father never spent much time on the playing field with myself compared to the time that some other fathers spent with their sons. Yet, in reviewing my years growing up, I never consider myself neglected. In fact, I know of few fathers who have given to their sons what my father gave me.

His way of paying back is hard to define as a formula; then again maybe reducing parenting to a formula is dangerous. What remains fixed in my mind are the memories of specific occasions where he showed his love, concern, and appreciation – instances where I felt my father pay back time that he had borrowed.

My first regular job in life was delivering newspapers. Growing up in Illinois meant the winters brought snow and sometimes plenty of it. One morning when I was eleven years old, I woke up at the usual four o'clock in the morning to commence delivery to the homes on my paper route. I remember this particular day being one of the coldest days on record. As much as I wished I could stay in bed, I knew this was not an option. The news had to go out despite the wind chill factor being forty degrees below zero fahrenheit.

As I was about to leave home on my bicycle, Dad came into the kitchen with a jacket pulled over his pyjamas. He said, "Wes I thought this morning it would be good to spend some time together. Why don't we hop in the car. We can talk while you get the news to your people." His profession never afforded him much opportunity to attend my school sport events but every now and then he would say, "Let's spend some time together."

I have recollections of many times like this one and I know there are many more that I've forgotten. What has never failed my memory was that he was a dad who paid back to the family what he borrowed – with interest. I aspire to do the same.

Pay Back What You Owe To Your Supporters

It is a marvelous experience to have someone success-ful turn around and give you some credit for their triumph. It may have been something you helped them with years ago. You thought it was nothing at the time. You may have even forgotten, but they haven't. Your phone call that came at a crucial time, the card of encouragement that you sent which helped them follow through to make that life changing momentous decision. Or that good word you put in for them, that risk you took on them, or that second mile you went with them. Whatever you did became light in their darkness.

We have all done this for others. Others have done it for us. Pause a moment and reflect upon those momentous turning points in your life. Often, there are people who help position us to experience the blessings of a turning point. Who are these people that have helped you? When was the last time you wrote to one of those people? Although it might be years after the event, receiving a letter of gratitude becomes a high point in anyone's day and gives them another entry for their victory book!

Having achieved a major triumph in you life, you get caught up in the glory and celebration of the victory. There is a little trap that positions itself at this point. As the celebration of victory subsides, you begin to get caught up with aspects of unwrapping the next dream. This process can sidetrack you from the realization that many people helped you gain the victory in the first place. When you are high on the thrill of a victory and hot on the tail of the next one, the last thing you tend to think about is the fact that we are not self made.

Call a 'time out' and spend some time distributing credit where credit is due. I know it's hard to find time when you are on a roll, but the repercussions of not doing so are devastating. On the other hand, credit distribution adds depth and meaning to the victory experience.

Firstly, to give credit where credit is due, acts as a reminder to you that you are not self made. This saves you from being seduced into believing that you are. Secondly, to give credit to someone makes them feel good about being a part of your pilgrimage instead of them feeling used by your pilgrimage. Thirdly, by example you inspire others to distribute gratefulness. It costs you little compared to what others have given you and in doing so, you rotate the wheel of inspiration. This gives humanity a wondrous uplift.

Pay Back What You Owe To The Bank

Nothing will stop you faster from becoming the person you dream of being than unserviceable debt.

Responsible debt is fundamentally good. That is, indebtedness to the bank for loans that help you purchase a home, something that produces income, an education, or a viable business. However, ultimately your income must match your outflow otherwise your upkeep becomes your downfall. Unserviceable debt leads you to crash financially and leaves you with your only asset being that you are richer for the experience. That is no fun and there are less traumatic ways of gaining this experience.

While some endure bankruptcy through unfortunate circumstances which were not the result of mismanagement, the sizeable proportion of people in this dilemma could have avoided it.

I have had the unfortunate experience of watching good people make poor decisions with regard to financing their dreams. The consequences for them are devastating.

111

Not only do they suffer under the great pressure that comes to bear, but it also cripples their spirit for a while. A period of their life is lost in recovery and it is a long time before they regain the desire to dream.

It is better to start very small at first. Don't expose yourself to being financially vulnerable. I am not saying don't take risks. What I am saying is don't bet all your worth on one hand. Build large scale success on smaller scale victories that keep increasing in size and building on one another. I appreciate the wisdom of Robert H. Schuller when he says, "Don't launch a rocket from a canoe".

There is no such thing as easy money. Most who go off in search of a killing, often do not return. Money is just that type of beast! Sure money can be a great servant but it makes a lousy lover. Respect it, and pay back what you borrow.

I am not an expert on financial affairs but what I do know is that nothing will stop you dead in your tracks more than financial problems. Pay attention to what comes in and what goes out. Success demands that some of that which flows in sticks with you. What flows out should never be the sum total of what came in, or worse, MORE than what came in!

Pay attention along your journey to the need to pay back what you borrow from the various banks, whether it be your body, your family, your friends, or your financial bank. Momentarily pause to give credit where credit is due, then continue the race with gusto. It is a long distance race my friends but for the ones who keep pace over the long haul there is joy indescribable.

❦

Irresponsible indebtedness can cripple your Dreams.

God
You - and your Body
your Family
your Friends
your Neighbors
your community
your Country
your Financial institutions

Banks
-what do you owe?
Pay it back with interest

CHAPTER EIGHT

Be Kind
Despite The Grind

RECENTLY I watched a music awards program on television. The compere was a well known and respected music artist. In the course of the evening, an award was won by a famous music band. Due to their involvement in a hectic touring schedule, the band was unable to attend the function to receive their award. Saved through the help of modern satellite technology, the viewers were able to see the band members accepting their award from another part of the world. They were sitting in a bar as the compere crossed 'live' to congratulate them. It was not long before the viewers realized that the band must have been seated at the bar for some time.

The compere was trying to extract something of value from the conversation, but try as he did, it was obvious these guys were not so much in another country as on another planet. What saddened me about the episode was how difficult they made it for the compere to save face. Whether their manner was alcohol or ego-induced, the result was the same: a display deficient of graciousness.

To be sure, the band had probably been working very hard. Maybe they were thirsty. I felt sorry for the event organizers who, as it turned out, had spent a great deal of money on satellite link-up only to be embarrassed.

Making it to the top is not an easy road. There are stresses and challenges that can wear away a person's patience and tolerance. There are many however, who rise to success maintaining civility and niceness throughout the journey. These great people prove that it is possible to BE KIND DESPITE THE GRIND.

When you are caught up in the grind, your patience is being tested by challenges and disappointments. It is inevitable that sometimes you will feel frustrated. While it is natural to vent some of this frustration, it is too easy to end up conveying an impression that you may later regret. You come away from such a situation thinking, "that's not the me I want the world to see." In fact, "it's not the me I want to be!" I regret having done it many times. Though I'm getting better, it still takes concerted effort to keep it out of the behavioural repertoire.

Every so often you meet a champion who is an ambassador of human kindness as well. These people inspire by their example. They give a good name to the word success. They stand testimony to the fact that you don't have to sacrifice noble character in order to achieve greatness. The truth is noble character is greatness.

What You Sow Is What You Grow

Some laws are part of the fabric of the universe. "You reap what you sow" is one such law. Like gravity, we have very little option apart from submitting to its authority. If you plant tomato seeds, you will harvest tomatoes. If you plant a gum nut seed, you'll grow a gum tree. I don't know of anyone who has come up with a way to defy this.

The law applies to us. If you sow criticism, you'll harvest criticism. If you sow encouragement, you'll reap encouragement. If you project gloom, the world will reflect doom. If you project hope, there will be hope reflected back to you. If you focus on failure, you will not be surprised when you find failure. If you plant goodness, you will raise a crop of good things.

Now, just because you make a concerted effort to be kind, don't suddenly think that the world will always be kind toward you. Sometimes it won't. There are people out there whose disposition is so hardened to humanity that they see you as a number and will treat you like a piece of machinery. Your kindness may not be responded to in the manner you deserve. But don't allow these people to drag you into their world of emotional numbness by becoming like them. Who knows, the light of your kindness might just shine through a crack in their hard exterior. You might be the only milk of human kindness that they ever taste. You may inspire them to start dreaming about the person they want to be!

There will be times when your patience is tested enormously. You will be the recipient of injustice. You will be treated unfairly. You will be prejudiced against. You will suffer because of the incompetence of others. To sum it up, there will be times when you deserve better. Oh yes, you will sure deserve better. Unfortunately, you don't always get what you deserve. Now, what are you going to do about it?

Some respond to unfair and unfortunate circum-stances in a kind way. They are more likely to gain more respect, friends, and usually get what they wanted in the first place. Some handle it a little more aggressively. They may get what they want but only if they trade respect and poten-tial friends in order to get it.

This reminds me of a fellow I once knew. At the slightest provocation of a raw deal, he would reach for his biggest guns to help sway the situation to his favour. Almost like calling in the National Guard, it was a powerful and intimidating technique. The problem was that it was a case of unnecessary overkill and resulted in his trail being littered with people harbouring ill will towards him. This was unfortunate because, when you got past the aggressive nature, he was a nice and talented guy with much to offer. Sad to say, his fiery disposition limited his potential in the long run.

There are a few problems with the "call in the National Guard" manner of operation. Usually the situation can be better resolved away from the shadow of the big guns. If a person recognizes they're under attack, they will immediately go on the counter attack in the name of self preservation. This often does nothing to resolve a situation but rather adds to the confusion.

Secondly, if the National Guard technique doesn't work, it's hard to use the nice approach when you've just, blown the other person's ship out of the water!

And finally, if there has been an honest mistake on the side of the perpetrator, reasoning in a kind way gives the person a chance to rectify the discrepancy. You have given them a chance to escape with their self esteem intact. They will appreciate you and respect you for it. You've made a friend because you have kept the focus on solving the problem rather than rousing on the person connected with the problem. Nobody likes being the recipient of a blasting. Besides, what is the use of getting it all your way if the process leaves you bankrupt in the relationship department.

One act of kindness ended up solving a major problem I had encountered. Many years ago, I was walking through our city mall. There was some construction taking place where a shop front was being remodelled. To enable themselves room to work, the builders had barricaded the main walkway. It meant people had to step up onto a grassy verge, walk about twelve paces, then step back down onto the pathway. This was fine for a spring chicken like myself. It was a problem, however, for the elderly lady I was walking behind. Her hands laden with shopping bags, I noticed she was having a difficult time navigating the detour. I should have been quicker to diagnose that this lady could have used my help. As she stepped down from the grassy verge, she lost her footing, fell, and landed on her face.

Though she could have done with my help before, there was no doubt she needed it now. Blood was pouring from her face. Being seventy or so years of age meant that her body could not make compensatory adjustments to minimize the severity of the fall. Consequently, her face literally took the impact. Time seemed to stand still. I saw about six builders stopped dead in their busy tracks, having seen that the barricade they had erected had contributed to this accident.

Taking out my clean white handkerchief, I compressed the handkerchief to the gash on her face in an attempt to slow down the flow of blood. There was a pharmacy next to the construction site and I figured someone in there would be able to help this lady. As the pharmacist was attending to the lady's injury, I felt a hand on my shoulder.

Turning around, the hand was connected to a man who introduced himself as the construction company foreman responsible for the work taking place next door.

He thanked me for my help and told me that he would take it from there. I told the elderly lady, who was still clutching my now blood stained handkerchief, that she was in good hands. As I left the pharmacy, I recall thinking, "Guess that's the last I see of my handkerchief!"

Four years later I was involved in the relocation project of a church. The leaders in charge were faced with the dilemma that their current location was no longer adequate. The lack of available seating and parking was actually discouraging further growth. It was decided that a new building be designed and erected. It was also decided that they relocate to a temporary building while the new one was being built.

The temporary building was a large, industrial warehouse. Let me tell you about the building complete in all its detail – concrete floor, concrete block walls, single sheet tin roof. That was it! All eleven thousand square feet of it. It gave very little by way of comfort except that it offered more room than what had been currently available to us.

My task was to furbish this concrete tent so that six hundred people could meet within its walls with a reasonable amount of comfort. Due to the cost of the new building construction, the advisers gave me a modest amount of ten thousand dollars to complete the transformation. Now this amount would be plenty if you were sprucing up a house. The problem was I was sprucing up Noah's ark!

I spent nine and a half thousand dollars on the construction of a platform, fire stairs, offices, book shop, restaurant, and school facilities. With the help of donated materials and volunteer labour, we were able to set in place all the provisions except one. I had eleven thousand square feet of concrete floor that desperately needed carpet, both to eliminate echo and reduce the effect of cold in the coming winter. Armed with my remaining five hundred dollars, I headed out to the carpet vendors in search of a very good deal.

The lowest quote for the cheapest carpet was forty thousand dollars! I looked at my five hundred dollars and the forty thousand dollar quote. I needed a miracle to happen. Something like when Jesus expanded five loaves and two fish to feed five thousand hungry people. Help!

The day for relocation was moving closer and still the floor-covering dilemma was yet to be solved. Pre-loved carpet, though half the price of new, was still forty times more than my remaining five hundred dollars. Vinyl was almost the cost of new carpet. In desperation, I even considered the possibility of gluing hessian or burlap material to the ground. Running out of options made me consider anything.

A few days later while in town, it came to my notice that there was a five floor building being refurbished. Sure enough, I saw a tradesman walk out the front door with a roll of carpet on his shoulder that he proceeded to throw into an industrial waste bin. My senses honed in on this possible breakthrough. I enquired of the tradesman as to the possibility of obtaining the unwanted carpet. He said he had no authority and that I should speak to the foreman who was located on the fifth floor.

The elevator door opened. Before me was a vast space, once the home of countless offices. The foreman, who was sitting at the only desk on the whole floor, heard the elevator doors open and walked toward me. I started my introduction speech which I had quickly thrown together while in the elevator. He interjected halfway through by saying, "I know you." I didn't recognize him at all, which put him at an advantage.

He proceeded to relay how he knew me: "About four years ago, my construction company was doing some work in the city mall. We were responsible for a barricade which lead to the unfortunate fall of an elderly lady. You were the guy who helped her into the pharmacy." The incident was lost amidst a stack of dust covered files in my mind. After a few moments it was found and I blew the dust off it.

He said that he hadn't known where to track me down to let me know that the lady was alright. Then he asked, "Now, what was it you wanted?" I quickly relayed our need for floor covering. He paused a moment then said, "You know, a group of solicitors have just bought this building. The present carpet wasn't their color choice so they asked us to dispose of it. I was apprehensive in disposing of it because, as you can see (giving it a kick with the toe of his boot), it still has a lot of life left in it."

Then he asked the forty thousand dollar question, "How much do you need?" I was a little embarrassed to tell him the truth. Throwing respectability out that fifth floor window, I drew a deep breath and told him, "Eleven thousand square feet."

He responded, "I have five floors of carpet and I would be pleased to give it to you. You'll find there's about fourteen thousand square feet in all."

I left that building uplifted. Not so much that I was given an enormous amount of carpet free of cost, but that his generosity was connected to a simple act of kindness I had done four years prior. I'd long forgotten it; he hadn't.

You are right. God didn't turn my five hundred dollars into forty thousand dollars but He did turn one handkerchief into fourteen thousand square feet of carpet!

You reap what you sow. It took four years. Nevertheless, that seed of kindness returned a bumper crop. It reminded me that being kind despite the grind not only helps others, but it comes back to you sooner or later.

❦

What goes around Comes around.

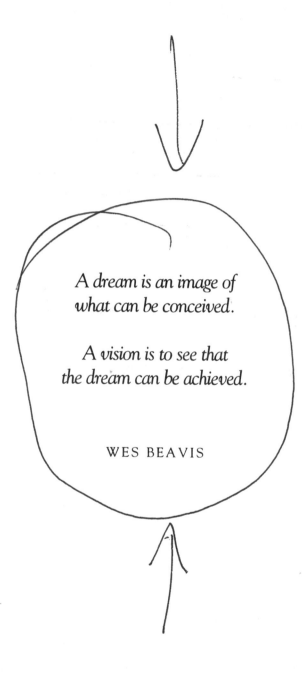

A dream is an image of
what can be conceived.

A vision is to see that
the dream can be achieved.

WES BEAVIS

CHAPTER NINE

Visionwork –
The Goal
And The Grunt

❦

GREAT ACHIEVEMENTS never eventuate by themselves. Sometimes I wish they would. Wouldn't it be
great if when you felt hungry for some self esteem to simply
go down to the PROUD ACHIEVEMENTS TAKE-AWAY
RESTAURANT and order a great achievement special? I
can just hear myself placing my order, "Can I have a promotion with a salary increase, a college degree, a medical
breakthrough, and a side order of the front cover on Time
Magazine to go? Oh, and can I have some extra applause
with that order?" What a world it would be; respectfully it is
not this world.

In this world, real greatness cannot be bought nor can
it be borrowed, and it certainly cannot be won. You see, the
price of greatness can only be paid with the currency of per-

sonal growth. Every growth experience on the road to becoming the person you dream of being transforms you into a greater person. Oliver Wendell Holmes, the Chief Justice of the United States Supreme Court at the turn of the century, was recorded saying: "Once a mind has been stretched by a new idea, it never returns to its original shape." The same can be said about our lives. When you are stretched by a new experience, you never return to your original size. You have become greater!

Greatness is your reward for having endured the struggles, survived the uncertainty, and persisted until a way was found. You are declared great because you overcame the cynicism, proved that it is possible, and inspired others to do the same. You are a person of greatness because you refused to accept less than what you dreamed possible. The journey to becoming the person you dream of being transforms you into what you dream of being – a person of greatness.

This is the reason why lottery winners, although rich in dollars, remain poor. They receive the prize without having invested the effort to gain the prize. It may be great to win the lottery, but the lottery win does not make you great. It is the investment of effort along the hard road of personal development which builds you to be great. It builds you to understand the prize and appreciate it, it builds you in the knowledge of what to do with the prize, it builds your strength to help others find their prize, and it builds you to be the person you dream of being.

Of all the dreams that come true, the sweetest are the ones which eventuate as the result of earnest deliberation and wholehearted conquest. They do not come true by accident, inheritance, luck, or merely good intentions. The treasures we esteem the most are a result of activity not passivity. One of my favourite sayings is: "All who sleep dream, but only those who work make their dreams come true."

Sometimes, one gets the feeling that work is the punishment for being alive. Work does not necessarily need to be viewed this way. Those who have savoured the harvest where they have sown realize that work can be the courier of a special kind of satisfaction; something that uplifts a person's self esteem. A satisfaction that inspires a person to consider even greater possibilities.

You ask, "How does cleaning our family bathroom week after week inspire me to greatness?" This is an acceptable question. Some work is not that inspirational. I won't try to convolute some principle benefit that springs out of cleaning the family toilet bowl, apart from the obvious. However, there is a type of work whereby the accomplishments bring huge rewards. Maybe even the scale of reward which allows you to retire from cleaning the bathroom for the rest of your life. This is a special type of work. It is called VISIONWORK.

Everyone has to work. It's one of those codes of the

universe. There is no such thing as a free lunch. Somebody's effort makes it possible. <u>We do not have a choice as to whether we will work or not.</u> It has already been made for us. <u>The good news is the type of work in which we engage our lives is entirely up to us.</u> Yes, that's right. <u>We get to choose what work we do!</u>

<u>It gets more exciting. There is a type of work out there which is so suited to your talents, giftedness, and dreams, and you will actually like the work.</u> You look forward to your next chance to engage in it. There are some people who actually begrudge having to break for meals and sleep because they enjoy their work so much. I am one of them.

Where do you find these jobs you ask? Well, it's not quite as simple as running down to your nearest employment agency and getting one. This type of work can be connected with a certain vocation but it is bigger than that. The work I speak of here is that work which makes a person feel as if they are accomplishing the purpose of their existence. This work will be found by discovering what your dreams are calling you to do and to be.

Now, this type of work is not synonymous with ease. In fact, it can be much harder. It involves times of pain, insecurity, sacrifice. Nonetheless, for the fulfilling satisfaction it brings, so many cherish the opportunity to keep in its employment long beyond retiring age.

I once thought the secret to a happy life was to avoid pain. I was wrong and have since realized the most satisfying happiness comes as a result of having endured pain. Visionwork is often painful. There are more comfortable ways to spend time than engaging in visionwork. While visionworkers don't like pain any more than anyone else, they are more readily accepting of it because it comes as part of the achievement process. They know that the joy of achieving something special requires sacrificing the comfort zone, but they are willing to do it because of the life expanding results it brings. That's why winners lead a life of subjecting themselves to the pain threshold. They know they cannot expand beyond their current experience unless they do so.

To take the easier option and avoid pain comes with an expensive price tag – never achieving one's vision. This is too high a price! To achieve your vision is paramount to the greatest feeling you'll ever have. It is a sad thing to miss out on the elation it brings. Winners endure pain because they love the rewards of having endured.

Let me be blatant about some personal feelings. I delight in immediate gratification. Sure I want the fun, the enjoyment, the satisfaction, and I'd prefer to have it now rather than waiting for later. However, I realize that to forgo some of the instant satisfaction today, I can fulfill a greater tomorrow; a tomorrow that brings with it dreams come true.

Visionwork is the work that you do which helps you achieve your goals. It's the work which you can see has a direct effect to helping you advance toward fulfilling the destiny of which you dream. When you drive to develop your dream, you are actively engaged in visionwork.

I find it very helpful to ask myself from time to time, "Is the activity, in which I'm presently engaged, in any way connected with the advancement towards the dream coming to reality?" Sometimes we get seduced into spending our time and energy on things that have no relationship with our dreams. While on some occasions the task maybe necessary, we must be careful that it doesn't leave us totally diverted from the goal.

The Goal
And The Grunt

There is nothing quite like the satisfaction of work, when you can feel it transporting you towards your goal. What brings the drudgery into activity is the lack of felt purpose for the activity. Whereas, if you have a meaningful reason for activity; if it relates to a reward you long for; if you know you are becoming greater as a person for your application, then you can give anything a great deal of effort. You are willing to sacrifice. You are willing to take a calculated chance. You are more willing to do whatever it takes; much more than if you had no goal providing real purpose.

Vision unlocks enthusiasm about the goal. Enthusiasm about the goal will inspire the grunt needed to get to the goal. That's good, because any goal worth striving for demands grunt. What is grunt? That quality of commitment that keeps you putting in the effort long after the thrill of the 'honeymoon' is gone. The people who have the greatest successes are not really the most talented, or educated, or capable, but rather those with a dream coupled with the drive to make it come true, A friend of mine puts it this way: "Vision gives birth to passion and passion puts the pleasure into effort."

Power For
The Darkened Hour

A vision has more power than an obstacle. A vision helps you outlast the obstacle. There will be days when you will feel whipped; days when something goes wrong in your plans; days wasted because something or someone has let you down; days of little progress, that leave you demoralized, wondering if your hopes will ever be realized. But these days do pass. Yes, the tide does go out but it also comes back in. Days which are gruelling will give way to days of greatness.

A vision keeps your focus forward whether you are swept up in successes or dogged by discouragement. If you are inspired by your vision, and if there is a way possible, then you will find that way. It may take time and it will take grunt but it will be worth it!

Midway through my teenage years, my family migrated from one country to another. Accordingly, it meant changing schools. In moving, I took the only transferable facet of my scholastic reputation with me – my school reports. Having settled in our new location, an appointment with the high school guidance counsellor was made to facilitate my starting at the new school. What began as a fairly insignificant meeting became the turning point in my attitude towards studies. It was also my first memorable experience of the power of visionwork.

I remember sitting in her office thinking admittance for my final two years of high school was little more than a paperwork formality. Sometimes one is wrong. This was one such example of my error in judgement.

Perusing my recent reports, she questioned my performance. She had every right to do so. I knew my academic prowess was not that clearly demonstrated by those reports. Having fun was not examinable. Disappointing really, because I demonstrated exemplary performance in that subject! After viewing my reports, the high school guidance counsellor proceeded to launch a missile in my direction. It caught me completely off guard.

She told me that due to my obvious inaptitude for studies, I should discontinue schooling and find a job.

What?! Not only was this the last thing I was expecting out of the interview, but I had assumed that it was every student's inalienable right to graduate from high school. This sentiment was not shared by the counsellor.

Suddenly, I found myself desperately trying to convince her of my suitability for continuing formal education. She conceded eventually to my pleading for the chance to prove myself, but reinforced her position by stating that I would probably not make it to Easter.

To a certain extent, the guidance counsellor was correct. The next two years were tough. I had a great deal to catch up with. Clawing back from the underdog position like this was not going to happen by sitting back and waiting for the challenger to drop the ball. It was solely dependent on personal drive.

Something in my great favour was that I had a dream to finish high school and a vision that beckoned me to prove the counsellor incorrect in her assumptions. The going was very difficult. So, partially she was right. What she had not taken into account however, was the dream factor. A dream to succeed, backed up with daily grunt, draws the possibility out of perceived impossibility.

I don't know if he invented the saying, but what Jesse Jackson once said is so true: "It's your attitude, not aptitude, which determines your altitude". Visionwork is all about the orientation of your attitude not your aptitude.

This is great news. Absolutely wonderful news! Once again you have been blessed with the ultimate power; the power to change your position by changing the way you think.

If the dream is worthy, honourable, courageous, and a blessing to others, you will be surprised to discover what is possible. For if it is possible, you can find a way if only you believe. Decide today to no longer surrender your life to something that is holding you back; holding you back from becoming the person of greatness that is, so far, only represented in your dreams.

Trading In Some Security For Some Adventure

Being involved in visionwork means you are on a course of adventure.

A good friend of mine was contemplating the possibility of pursuing a line of work he had always dreamed of doing. Though he was experiencing a great deal of security and success in his current position, it wasn't ultimately what he wanted to do with his life. To pursue the dream however, meant he would have to relinquish some security. That's the price of adventure; if you want more adventure in your life you have to trade in some security to get it.

My friend sought the counsel of someone older and wiser when faced with an opportunity to do something he had always dreamed of doing. The tension my friend was facing was that it meant resigning from a well paid job. The advice he was given was: "It doesn't matter how much money you make. Even if you become a millionaire. If you never take a shot on what you believe you've been put on the planet to do, you'll live a life of regret, living in the shadow of wondering what could have been."

In 1972 my parents sold almost every possession they owned. Any thing which represented security ended up on the alter of adventure. What an adventure! It has made me what I am today. With four children, aged six, eight, ten, and twelve, they boarded a ship bound for a country on the other side of the world. Radical? Yes. Nonsensical? Yes. Scary? Yes. My father had no job lined up. The only point of security was the name and address of a family who were prepared to house us until my father found a job.

When we arrived in the new town, the local paper wanted to write a story on our family. The newspaper reporter arrived with his photographer. My part was easy – pose for a family photo. It ran in the newspaper the following day. Headlining the story were the words: "After Nine Years – Couple's Dream Comes True." I remember reading that and thinking that my parents were strange to let a dream compel them to transport the family across the world. I remember wishing that they had a real reason for the move like a job transfer or something.

I have come to more than appreciate what they did. I am inspired by it. I can't think of any better motivation. They had a dream and were willing to move out of the comfort zone to make the dream come true. They could have waited all their lives for someone to hand them the opportunity. They decided to make their own. The price was high. A great deal of security was sacrificed, but we were repaid with life changing adventure.

Forever, I will be grateful for their gift.

Position Yourself To Catch The Wind When It Blows

Visionwork takes on many forms. One of them is what I call positioning. Sometimes, the work we do is to help move us into a better position of readiness for when the desired opportunity comes along – a means to an end. Universities, colleges, and schools all represent visionwork situations which assist a person in positioning. There are other ways to position yourself which are not institutionally based. The experience of a friend of mine is one such example.

Mark worked for a major security company. As head of a computer department, his task was to assist his company organize themselves to be taken over by a British based company. The buy-out also involved the annihilation of many of his present company's departments including his own. In short, he was setting up his own loss of job.

While the thought of being on vocational death row was not a sweet one, there was a positive side. The take-over was not set to take place for a few years. This was fortunate. It gave him time to consider the possibilities and devise a plan of action. The inevitable job loss turned out to be one of his greatest blessings.

You see, while Mark was very capable with computers, it was not what he ultimately wanted to do with his life. His dream was to become a police officer. He used the time to find out how to enter a new career in law enforcement.

His research highlighted the fact that admittance into the force was not going to be easy as openings were not readily available and at best, difficult to obtain. When a position did come up, the high number of applications was enough to discourage even the most self-assured. So Mark decided to position himself better to increase his chances of being noticed when the opportunities arose.

While continuing his computer job, he took on a second job in a voluntary capacity. He became what is called an auxiliary volunteer police officer. It largely comprised of minor duties such as directing traffic. Not a glamorous start to say the least, but it gave him a better positioning. While performing these voluntary duties, he became acquainted with the officers in charge and gave them the opportunity to get to know him.

This volunteer position worked out to be a three hour shift per day on top of his regular job. How long did this go on for? Many weeks? No. A few months? No. A whole year? No, his break came five years later. Three thousand hours of voluntary work preceded his professional appointment.

Mark graduated from the police academy and has been serving as an officer with merit for exemplary service ever since. He has done what police officers do best, save lives. My pride in him swells when I hear of commendation awards in his honour. I am just as proud of the way he positioned himself to catch the opportunity when it came by. He set his sails to catch the wind when the wind blew.

It was hard for his family. It meant they had to go without many things that other families were enjoying. They were willing to delay the gratification for the sake of a greater tomorrow. When that greater tomorrow came, it brought with it a capacity to make up for the sacrifices which had to be made on the drive towards the dream.

Visionwork Saves You From Cynicism

The greater the dream, the tougher it is to gain. It is very easy to feel that achieving the goal is impossible. Some succumb to staying in an unfavoured position because they do not have the drive or the vision to change their lot in life. They are entitled the freedom to be this way. What is unfortunate is that people in this state of self imposed exile sometimes become cynical and judgmental. One of the great things about visionwork is that it keeps you occupied on a task which gives you hope. Hope, in turn, has a way of eradicating cynicism.

You will notice that successful people are people of hope. It reflects in their attitude, their posture, their reticence to enter into the world of criticism. They realize that to criticize costs time and energy, and pays nil in return. They know that nobody ever erects a monument in honour of a critic. In short, they know it is a poor investment.

When you are caught up in the exciting flight towards your destiny, it lifts your spirit above those things which can hold you down. It's not that you haven't got reason to be negative, critical, and judgmental. You may have more reason than most! The drive towards your dream will be fraught with disappointments and injustice. You will have more than enough reason to be negative. Yet, you choose not to be negative. You avoid the alluring invitation to lay back in the arms of the seductress called cynicism. You know to entertain her will sap you of valuable time and energy – resources which the dream achiever devotes to winning the prize.

❦

CHAPTER TEN

Take Hold Of Someone's Hand

❦

I T IS ALWAYS a special time of television viewing when the Olympics are on. In the 1992 Barcelona Olympics in Spain, an incident took place that I will never forget. It was a men's sprint race. An Afro-English sprinter named Derek Redmond was lined up in the starting blocks with the rest of the contenders for Olympic glory. The signal sounded and the race began.

With fury and determination, the sprinters ran this race of their lives before a billion eyes around the world. Then tragedy struck. Derek Redmond buckled over under the agony of a torn hamstring. For Derek, the race was over.

At the finish line, a great crowd of officials surrounded the race finishers. Positions were being decided. Derek remained alone on the track where the injury struck anguishing, both physically and mentally. Then the greatest spectacle happened that I have ever seen in Olympic competition. To me, far greater than the awarding of a medal, displaying more honour than carrying the Olympic torch, and more moving than the sound of one's own national anthem being played.

Derek was still in the running lane buckled over in pain. His father, Jim Redmond, walked onto the track and threw his arms around his son. Not caring that he was being watched by people the world over, he gave support in his son's moment of desperate need.

Holding on to each other, they made their way towards the finish line. "We're going to finish this race together," Jim was heard to say. As they did, they reminded us that we are not so great as to never need someone to lean on.

Indeed, one of the most important factors of the human pilgrimage is the realization that we were never meant to journey alone.

Turning The Wheel Of Inspiration

Have you ever walked away from a person feeling richer for having experienced their presence? If you have, you've experienced the power of someone turning the wheel of inspiration. Have you ever been in need of a hand and someone stopped to help you? Again, if you have, you've experienced the power of someone turning the wheel of inspiration.

You know when you have taken a ride on the wheel of inspiration when you feel uplifted by someone around you. Sometimes these people come in the form of life long friends, other times they can be brief encounters where names are not even exchanged.

One such experience for me was at the Los Angeles International Airport. My plane for Sydney was due to leave in an hour. Having checked in my luggage, I proceeded to pay for my departure tax. My recollection from travelling in and out of the United States a few years previously was that departure tax costs fifteen dollars. Not wanting to leave the country with unspent US currency, I made sure that I spent it all bar the fifteen dollars needed for the tax. I tucked that carefully into the back of my wallet knowing it, along with my air ticket, was all I needed to get out of the country.

It came time when the check-in lady asked for my departure tax payment. Feeling clever about producing my last fifteen dollars, I placed it on the counter, right next to the sign that read 'Departure Tax – $18.00'. Reading the sign induced the feeling that my heart had stopped.

Checking in at an airport which deals with one hundred thousand passengers per day is enough of an experience. The last thing I needed, having already waited a long time in a queue, was to interrupt the baggage check-in process with an unscheduled trip to the foreign exchange counter, wherever that was!!

Wondering how I would make up the extra three dollars, I reached for my change wallet hoping that I had a healthy supply of coins left. Two dollars and a few pennies. Not enough. Sensing defeat, I turned to the check-in lady and informed her of my predicament. Then, an amazing thing happened.

Standing next to her was a six foot tall young man called Terrance. His job was to help her lift the heavier luggage on to the conveyer belt. Seeing my predicament, he reached into his pocket and pulled out a dollar bill and put it on the counter next to my inadequate amount. Terrance smiled and said it was his pleasure to help me out.

I couldn't believe it. This was Los Angeles! The home of riots, freeway shootings, and car jackings. Yet, it was also the home of Terrance, a man who with a one dollar gesture of kindness taught me that there is still love in that city.

You could assume that organizing one hundred thousand people would dehydrate airport staff of the milk of human kindness. It probably does. But for one moment, by giving a complete stranger a dollar, Terrance TURNED THE WHEEL OF INSPIRATION. Something tells me that Terrance is headed for amazing greatness.

It's wonderful to receive this lift from the wheel but it's just as wonderful, and even more important, to stop and turn the wheel for someone else. It takes little more than some thoughtfulness to pass on to others, the lift that has been passed on to you.

Every time you pause to help elevate another's life you provide inspiration to them. On your journey to becoming the person you dream of being, don't miss out on this wonderful experience. Turn that wheel! Indeed it can be the very factor bringing a greater degree of satisfaction to your success.

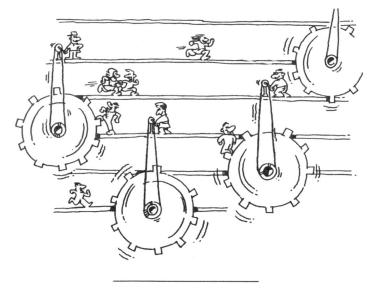

Passing It On

Is our dream to be great an end in itself? Is that why we achieve something significant so we can sit back and say look at me, I'm so great? If we are honest, we all like to be noticed and considered to be special, but personal greatness encumbers something more noble than that. Personal greatness turns the wheel of inspiration. When the wheel turns, it lifts up those who come under its influence.

Part of your pilgrimage to greatness will involve building others. This is what adds the fulfilling dimension to your endeavors. You achieving your dream can spin off great blessings to people around you, and even those you will never meet. When someone tells me that my efforts have helped change their life for the better, it's a precious moment. To think that pursuing my dream would actually have the side effect of lifting others, beside myself, to greatness – will wonders ever cease? Not for those driving toward their dream!

At fourteen years of age, I was in the office of my youth group leader. His name was Philip. The reason why I was there has not survived in my memory, but the memory of something that happened in that office will survive forever. The phone rang. Philip answered it and engaged in a lengthy conversation. Standing in the corner of his office was his guitar. As a means of passing the time, I picked it up and tried to get a tune out of it. The best I could do was an unrecognizable, one string version of 'Smoke On The Water'. Philip, while still engaged in the phone conversation, took notice of how I had become consumed in my musical activity.

Finishing the phone conversation, he turned to me and asked if I had ever considered playing the guitar. Philip played the guitar well and I admired how this talent added to my perception of his great persona. In my adolescent-induced lack of self confidence, I indicated a desire but also feelings of apprehension as to whether I had the talent needed to learn. Sweeping my apprehension aside with one compliment about his belief in me, he proceeded to give me my first guitar lesson.

On that day Philip released dormant potential. He set me on the course to achieving a career in music. That day, Philip turned the wheel of inspiration. Today, I get many letters, mostly from people I have never met, telling me what my music has meant to them. Sometimes when I listen to an album I've recorded, or hear a crowd of thousands sing one of my songs, I recall the day that Philip took a half-hour break in his day to PASS ON the gift he had, to me.

The wheel of inspiration lifted me to what I am today. I count it a privilege to keep that wheel turning. You can help spin that wheel as well. More than ever, this world is in need of people who can turn that wheel.

There is so much unrealized potential wrapped up in people who just need a helping hand to get started. On the way to achieving your dreams, you can help boost-start others.

Sometimes, all a person needs is not that much. Most times, what people are longing for is someone to affirm them. I remember a successful business couple once saying, that they owed their start to someone who believed in them long before they had reason to believe in themselves.

There have been times these simple words: "You've got what it takes, I believe you are going to be great", is all that is needed to rescue a person into fulfilling their potential. It is as if your belief in someone shines a light into the darkness of their state of no confidence. Your light gives them hope that there could still be something out there. It inspires them to take a step. Regardless of how insecure that step, it is a step towards fulfilling their potential.

The wonderful thing is that you can affect people this way in the course of your journey. It rarely costs you anything significant, and it gives a fulfilling dimension to the evolution of greatness in your life. Thus, the wheel of inspiration turns again. Humanity is lifted up one more notch.

No, personal greatness is never an end in itself. It was never meant to be. Those who have turned the wheel of inspiration know that there is nothing like the satisfaction of looking back on their pilgrimage and noticing people benefitting by the trail they have made.

Wouldn't you like that as your own testimony? To see your move forward creating a wake of energy that envelopes others, lifting them up towards their own greatness. To have the experience of someone giving honour to you for helping them escape their black hole. To feel like others are also experiencing the blessing of your dreams come true. To wonder how many people caught up in your wake will go on to create their own. To consider the millions who could be richer because you dared to reach into darkness and take hold of someone's hand.

Isn't it fantastic? Not only will your dream change you and grant you greatness, it will also make this world a better place to live.

My friend, someone out there will be inspired to become the person they dreamed of being, because they admire how you dared to become the person you dreamed of being. Go for greatness. Friend, go for greatness. So many will be enriched because of you. The world stands in need of you to become the person you dream of being.

❦

If your desire is your dream
And you're determined to get through
Your dreams can be your destiny
For dreams do come true

WES BEAVIS

When We Believe

To live this moment through, spending it with you
I know will do us good
And I just want to say, Lord knows I pray
That our dreams come true

When we believe, we can find a way and we will make it
When we believe, we become a light in darkened places
And we can reach into the darkness
And take hold of someone's hand
When we believe, we become a light brightening our land

And until the end, I'll run with you my friend
Together we'll defend
And we will run with hope, this is how we'll cope
And on our dreams depend

When we believe, we can find a way then we will make it
When we believe we become a light in darkened places
And we can reach into the darkness
And take hold of someone's hand
When we believe, we become a light brightening our land

ABOUT THE AUTHOR

WES BEAVIS is a songwriter, performer, and speaker. He was born in Perth, Australia but migrated to the United States at age ten where he lived in Peoria, Illinois. On his return to Australia, he obtained a Bachelors degree in Theology and pastored one of Australia's largest churches. He now travels extensively in the capacity of motivational entertainer and communicator.

Living south of Sydney, Wes is married to Eleanor who accomplishes the amazing balancing feat of being a mother and high school teacher.

You've Read his Book, now Listen to his Songs!

Ten inspiring songs to motivate you!

WES BEAVIS — WHEN WE BELIEVE

ORDERED BY	
ADDRESS	
CITY	STATE
POSTCODE	TELEPHONE

Mail to : POWERBORN
PO Box 192, Figtree NSW Australia 2525
Telephone (042) 72 1411
or Fax to : (042) 71 6383
Guarantee : Simple, if you don't like it – send it back within 10 days please.
Orders from outside Australia : make Bank Draft payable in Australian Currency.

HOW MANY	ITEM	DESCRIPTION	PRICE EACH	TOTAL PRICE
	CASSETTE	WES BEAVIS – WHEN WE BELIEVE	AUS$18.95	$
	CD	WES BEAVIS – WHEN WE BELIEVE	AUS$27.95	$

Method of Payment :
☐ CHEQUE or POSTAL ORDER ☐ BANKCARD
☐ MASTERCARD ☐ VISA
CARD No. EXPIRATION DATE ☐☐–☐☐
☐☐☐☐☐ ☐☐☐☐☐ ☐☐☐☐☐ ☐☐☐☐☐
SIGNATURE REQUIRED WITH ALL CREDIT CARDS
X _____

SUB-TOTAL	$
POSTAGE & PACKAGING	$

1 CD OR CASSETTE ADD $3
MORE THAN 1 – WE PAY!

TOTAL	$